Uncle John's
BATHROOM
READER.

Horse Lover's
Companion

Uncle John's
BATHROOM READER

Horse Lover's
Companion

PORTABLE
PRESS

Bathroom Readers' Institute
San Diego, California, and Ashland, Oregon

Some of the stories included in this edition have been reprinted or
excerpted from the following *Bathroom Reader* titles: *Uncle John's
Ahh-Inspiring Bathroom Reader, Uncle John's Bathroom Reader Plunges
Into History Again, Uncle John's Bathroom Reader Plunges into National
Parks*, and *Uncle John's Bathroom Reader Plunges into Texas*.

"Bathroom Reader," "Portable Press," and "Bathroom Readers'
Institute" are registered trademarks of Baker & Taylor, Inc.
All rights reserved.

For information, write The Bathroom Readers' Institute
Portable Press, 10350 Barnes Canyon Road, Suite 100,
San Diego, CA 92121
e-mail: unclejohn@btol.com

ISBN 13: 978-1-59223-911-5
ISBN 10: 1-59223-911-0

Library of Congress Cataloging-in-Publication Data

Uncle John's bathroom reader horse lover's companion.
    p. cm.
 ISBN-13: 978-1-59223-911-5 (hardcover)
 1. Horses—Miscellanea. 2. Horses—Humor. I. Bathroom Readers'
Institute (Ashland, Or.)
 SF301.U57 2008
 636.1—dc22

                                    2008017985

Printed in Canada
First printing: September 2008

08 09 10 11 12   10 9 8 7 6 5 4 3 2 1

Contents

Helping Hands

Tack and Feed

Island Equines

Horses in the Wild West

Fame and Fortune

Horsing Around

The Winners' Circle

Puzzles and Quizzes

Horses in History

Did You Know?

A Breed Apart

Mixed Bag

Tails to Inspire

Entertaining Equines

Thank You!

The Bathroom Readers' Institute sincerely thanks the following people whose hard work and assistance made this book possible.

Gordon Javna

JoAnn Padgett

Melinda Allman

Amy Miller

Julia Papps

Jeff Altemus

Michael Brunsfeld

Dan Mansfield

Bonnie Vandewater

Art Montague

Debbie Hardin

J. Carroll

John Hogan

Julie Sartain

Kerry Kern

Lea Markson

Jenness Crawford

Megan Kern

Myles Callum

Sue Steiner

Katie Jones

Sydney Stanley

Monica Maestas

Lisa Meyers

Amy Ly

Kait Fairchild

Ginger Winters

Cynthia Francisco

Duncan McCallum

Bea and Sophie

Hey, Horse Lovers!

While we were working on the next book in our animal-lovers series, we caught sight of something amazing: a horse named Big Brown looked like he was about to win the Triple Crown. That hadn't happened since a gallon of gas cost 63 cents and less than 10 percent of Americans owned microwave ovens. (That was 1978, when Affirmed won it.)

Big Brown ended up not capturing the historic title, but the hoopla and excitement reminded us of how much we love horses. So why not write a book about them?

That was all the folks at the Bathroom Readers' Institute needed to start researching and writing, tracking down the most magnificent marvels in the equisphere and packing them into these pages. Here are some of the things they found out for you:

- Mr. Ed's backstage secrets.

- How horses inspired the creation of the ASPCA.

- Why horses are mounted on the left.

- The history of saddles, stirrups, and feed.

- Rowdy tales of rodeo's rough-and-tumble riders.

- How to work a dude ranch . . . in Australia and Argentina.

- The ins and outs of reining.

- Why velvet hardhats have a bow in the back.
- The short, spectacular story of the pony express.

And of course, we couldn't leave out horse racing. There's the mighty Man o' War, Secretariat the superstar, stories of grooms and jockeys, the number of roses in the Kentucky Derby blanket, and a lot more.

Whether you're an experienced rider or just learning about horses, you'll find plenty of facts, stories, and trivia about humans' most useful animal friend. So settle down in the tack room and get ready for a great ride.

And as always, go with the flow . . .

—Uncle John and the BRI Staff

The Horse Whisperers' Secrets

*"And I whispered to the horse; 'Trust no man in whose
eye you do not see yourself reflected as an equal.'"*
—Poet Don Vincenzo Giobbe

When horse power drove the world, there was plenty of work for anyone who could tame a wild mustang or rehabilitate a horse who turned hostile. Most trainers followed traditional, and sometimes painful, methods that used force to "break" a horse and make it submit. But there were always legends about people who understood horses so well that they could gain the animals' trust and cooperation through mutual respect. These legends went back hundreds of years, and often such horsemen were thought to have magical powers.

The Secret Method

In 350 BC, Greek philosopher Xenophon wrote *On Horsemanship*. His wasn't the first text on working with horses—that honor goes to a Mesopotamian horse trainer named Kikkuli, who wrote a book around 1400 BC. But Xenophon's work was the most comprehensive, and it emphasized training through kindness and reward rather than force. In modern times, a 19th-century Irishman named Daniel Sullivan rehabilitated dangerous horses using his own "secret" method: Sullivan stayed alone in a barn for a few hours with a vicious or terrified horse, and when he led the animal out, it would be calm and well mannered. No one knows Sullivan's secret for sure, but some people noticed that when he worked with a horse, he faced the animal as if preparing to speak to it. So he earned the nickname "the horse whisperer."

A "Rarey" Tradition

Sullivan died in 1810, but a few horsemen carried on his work. The most famous was John Solomon Rarey of Grovesport, Ohio. Rarey started taming horses on his father's farm when he was 12 and worked out his own method without spurs, whips, or force. He became so suc-cessful that he gained a reputation as a man who could

break the most difficult animals—he even tamed a team of elk. When word of Rarey's "horse whispering" reached England's Queen Victoria in 1858, she summoned him to

Windsor Castle and asked him to tame her husband's dangerous charger. Rarey spent some time with the charger in his stall. All was eerily quiet, so after a few minutes, the worried queen and her entourage peeked inside and saw the horse lying side-by-side with Rarey, who was using the animal's hind legs as a pillow.

On the Road

With Queen Victoria as a reference, Rarey traveled the world taming horses (and even a zebra). His most famous triumph was the rehabilitation of Cruiser, a stud stallion who had killed two grooms. Cruiser wore an iron muzzle and had to be fed through a funnel so as not to injure the stable boys. But it took Rarey only three hours to make Cruiser docile enough that (the *New York Times* later reported) he could be "fondled like a kitten."

Rarey became a celebrity. His book, *The Complete Horse Tamer*, was a best seller and explained his secret: Rarey painlessly hobbled one of the horse's legs with a special strap he'd invented himself. Standing on just three legs quickly tired the horse so that Rarey could make it lie down. Then he gently overwhelmed and calmed the animal with strokes and petting and by speaking in low, soothing tones. The result was a horse who trusted and obeyed him.

"Zen Master of the Horse World"

More than a century after Rarey's death, British author Nicholas Evans wrote *The Horse Whisperer*, a best-selling novel about a horse named Pilgrim who was horribly injured in an accident. In 1998, the book became a movie starring Robert Redford as Tom Booker, the horse whisperer who rehabilitates Pilgrim.

According to Evans, Tom Booker's skill with horses was inspired by the accomplishments of real people. One was Rarey—in the movie, Booker uses the Rarey strap technique to gentle Pilgrim. But the primary inspiration for the book was a modern horse whisperer from Wyoming named Dan "Buck" Brannaman.

Like John Rarey, Brannaman started training horses at 12, and his methods don't include punishment or pain. After watching Buck Brannaman help traumatized horses, Evans had these admiring words: "His skill, understanding, and his gentle, loving heart have parted the clouds for countless troubled creatures. Buck is the Zen master of the horse world."

What Makes 'Em Kick?

According to Brannaman, part of his knowledge comes from hard-won horse sense. After being bitten, bucked, and run over, he decided he'd do better if he could understand what made horses tick . . . as well as kick. So Brannaman studied "natural horsemanship," a tradition that takes its cues from a horse's instincts and innate methods of communication.

Natural horsemanship encourages trainers to "listen to horses" by understanding the animals' herd instincts and body language and then use that information to communicate in a way the horses understand. A "natural horseman," for example, will use the horse's herd instincts to maintain leadership. With the trainer acting as the head of the herd, he gains the animal's trust and cooperation. Brannaman, who himself was abused as a child, especially likes to work with mistreated animals. He's sensitive to their psychology and uses "patience, leadership, compassion, and firmness" to help them overcome their traumatic pasts.

Buck Brannaman has also become a motivational speaker teaching others to use horse-whispering techniques to help troubled children and adults. Teaching horse whispering as a philosophy, Brannaman says, "For me, these principles are really about life, about living your life so that you're not making war with the horse, or with other people."

* * *

The Ancients

Horses first appeared in cave art about 30,000 years ago. The animals weren't domesticated then, but they were clearly a part of life for early humans. Even though there's a lot of disagreement about when horses were domesticated (and very little solid evidence), most archaeologists believe that horses began living with people in Eurasia around 6,000 years ago.

You Know You're a Horse Person When . . .

Think you've got horse fever? Here are a few warning signs.

- You lean forward when your car goes over speed bumps.
- You yell at the kids, and the horse's name pops out.
- "Stopping by the stable" takes a minimum of two hours.
- You tell the guy at the service station that you've got a leak in the "near hind" tire.
- You feel a sharp spot on your back teeth and wonder if they need to be floated.
- You find hay in your bathrobe.
- You cluck at your car when it goes up hills.
- You know more about your horse's ancestry than your own.
- You carry a hoof pick in your purse.
- You've been banned from the laundromat.
- You refer to your shins as "cannon bones."
- After it snows, the first thing that gets shoveled is the path to the manure pile.
- You spend hundreds of dollars to compete in a horse show for a 98-cent ribbon.

6

Just the Stats

Get to know horses by the numbers.

¼ to ⅜ inch
Length a horse's hoof grows in a month.

1 hour
On average, the amount of time it takes for a foal to stand up and walk after it's born.

2
Blind spots for a horse: directly behind, and directly in front.

4 inches
One hand.

9 pounds
Weight of a horse's heart.

10 gallons
Amount of saliva a horse produces every day. One horse can also drink about 10 gallons of water and eat 15 to 18 pounds of hay each day.

18 feet
Longest horse mane, grown by a mare named Maude.

20 to 30 years
A horse's average life span.

36
Number of teeth adult female horses have. Adult male horses have between 40 and 44.

100°F to 101°F
A horse's normal body temperature.

335 to 340 days
Length of the horse's gestation period. On average, colts spend a week longer in the womb than fillies.

350 degrees
A horse's field of vision. Horses have the largest eyes of any land mammal. Their vision is monocular—each eye acts independently. (A human's field of vision is only about 140 degrees.) Horses have sharper vision than dogs or cats.

58 million
Number of horses living in the world today. At 8 million, China has the largest population. The United States is fourth with about 7 million horses.

The Bandit Queen

*Here's how horse theft became the family business for one
of the Wild West's most notorious female outlaws.*

The wanted poster read "Cattle and Horse Thief,"
listed her aliases as "unknown," and identified her
crime (among others) as heading a band of rustlers in
Oklahoma. So began the legal trouble for Belle Starr,
nicknamed the "Bandit Queen."

The Makings of an Outlaw

Ornery was in her blood. Her father, John, ran an inn,
and her mother, Eliza, was related to the infamous
Hatfield family—of Hatfields and McCoys fame. Starr was
born Myra "Belle" Shirley in Carthage, Missouri, in 1848.
Young Belle went to a fancy private school in Carthage
where she learned Latin, Greek, math, and even how to
play the piano.

The Shirleys were Confederate sympathizers (John
Shirley owned several slaves), and one of their sons was
killed during the Civil War. Belle aided the Confederacy
during the war, too—the teenager spied on and reported
back about Union troops. It was during this time that she
made her first illicit connections: she met outlaw Cole
Younger, his brothers, and Jesse and Frank James.

Becoming the Bandit Queen

Eventually, the Shirley family moved to Texas, where Belle married a farmer named Jim Reed. The couple had two children: Pearl (there are rumors her father was really Cole Younger) and Ed. There wasn't much money in farming, though, so Jim Reed began working with the Youngers, the James brothers, and a cattle-and horse-thieving Cherokee clan called the Starrs. Over the next three years, Jim Reed robbed stagecoaches, killed at least one person, and went on the run with his family. The police suspected Belle was in on the crimes, too—she started gambling in saloons, wearing a Stetson, and carrying pistols, which added to her outlaw image. But there was never any direct evidence that she helped her husband. Still, when Jim was killed by a sheriff's deputy, Belle took his place in the Starr clan. (She sent the kids to live with relatives.)

New Husband, Old Problems

Here's where the story gets murky. In 1880, Belle married Sam Starr, and by some accounts, she became the brains behind the family's criminal operations—in particular, horse thievery and cattle rustling. Others paint Belle as a victim of circumstance . . . a woman who fell in with the wrong crowd and just wanted to "live out [her] time in peace."

Either way, both Belle and Sam were soon caught and charged with horse theft, cattle rustling, and various other crimes. Finally, they ended up before Texas's notorious

Isaac "Hanging Judge" Parker, who sentenced them to one year in prison. (They each served nine months.)

Blast From the Saddle

The time in jail didn't halt Belle's criminal activities. In fact, she continued to be part of the Starr family business even after Sam was killed in a gunfight in 1886. Her next husband and her teenage son were also both indicted for horse stealing during the 1880s.

Finally, in February 1889, her outlaw life caught up with her. After a shopping trip alone (her husband was at the county courthouse facing yet another horse-stealing charge), Belle rode home. But before she arrived, a mysterious shotgun blast from the woods beside the road threw Belle from her saddle. Her spooked horse raced back to the Starr house, and his arrival alerted Belle's daughter Pearl, who went looking for her mother. But the Bandit Queen's story was over. Belle Starr was dead just two days before her 41st birthday. Her killer was never caught.

* * *

Horsey Happy Birthday

January 1 is the universal birthday for all horses registered in North America, no matter when during the year they were actually born.

The Great Meddler's Cause

*Today, the American Society for the Prevention of Cruelty
to Animals is known mostly for its work with dogs and cats.
But its origin is tied to one man's horror at the treatment
of New York City's working horses.*

In the 1860s, many city horses lived miserable lives.
They worked until they dropped, were underfed and
habitually beaten, and rarely had enough water to drink.
A working horse's average life span was just two to four
years. And horses who were too old or sick to work were
often turned loose in the streets to die.

Enter the Great Meddler

Henry Bergh was the son of a wealthy shipbuilder and
mostly led a life of leisure. He went to Columbia
University (but didn't graduate) and then worked for his
father's shipyard. But when his father died in 1843, Bergh
sold the business, collected his inheritance, and moved to
Europe for a while with his wife. By the 1860s, he was
back in New York with little to do.

In 1863, President Abraham Lincoln sent Bergh to
Russia as an ambassador to the court of Czar Alexander II.

(The Bergh family had long-standing connections in American politics.) It was there that he first noticed the inhumane treatment of animals. In particular, Bergh noticed that the Russian peasants often mistreated the horses pulling their *droshkies* (carriages), and he became incensed at humans' cruelty toward animals.

Two years later, on his way back to the United States, Bergh visited London. There, he met with the Earl of Harrowby, president of the Royal Society for the Prevention of Cruelty to Animals. Founded in 1824, the society was devoted to animal welfare (initially cattle, but later all animals), and it was from this model that Bergh came up with the idea to start a similar group in the United States.

"A Matter Purely of Conscience"

Initially, Bergh focused his attention on New York City's working horses. First, he organized a group of supporters: everyone from the minister at his church to local businessmen. They began pressuring the New York legislature to pass a law making it illegal for a person to beat, starve, or otherwise neglect an animal in his care.

In the meantime, Bergh founded the American Society for the Prevention of Cruelty to Animals (ASPCA). When asked why he was devoting so much of his time to this cause, he replied, "This is a matter purely of conscience; it has no perplexing side issues. It is a moral question in all its aspects."

The First Rescue

In 1866, Bergh spoke before the New York State Legislature and gave them his proposal. He referred to "these mute servants of mankind" and cited the many ways in which animals were being abused. The lawmakers were so moved by his speech that they passed a law incorporating the ASPCA and banning the mistreatment of animals. They also gave the newly formed society the right to enforce the new anti-cruelty law.

Three days later, Bergh saved his first animal when he came upon a New York City carriage driver beating his emaciated horse. A crowd gathered as Bergh, wearing a top hat and badge, reprimanded the man, unhitched the horse, and led it away.

Newspapers picked up the story, and debate began. Some people called Bergh "the great meddler"; others considered him an angel. Over time, the ASPCA's emblem took on the latter incarnation: an avenging angel, armed with a sword, stepping between a man and a mistreated wagon horse. Bergh continued to work with the group for the rest of his life.

ASPCA Innovations

In its first 100 years, the

ASPCA introduced many animal-friendly innovations, some of which are still used today:

- In 1867, the society used the first ambulance for injured horses—drawn by a horse.
- In 1875, Bergh invented a sling to lift horses who had difficulty getting up.
- The same year, he invented a mechanical pigeon for sport shooting so live birds no longer had to be used.
- In 1894, the ASPCA opened the first animal shelters and started issuing dog licenses.
- In 1902, ASPCA ambulances became mechanized— two years before human ambulances did.
- In 1912, the ASPCA opened its first veterinary hospital, which treated all animals for free. The hospital focused primarily on treating horses, but it didn't turn away other animals.
- ASPCA vets also pioneered the use of anesthesia for animals, and in 1961, they performed the first open-heart surgery on a dog.

The ASPCA Today

Henry Bergh died in 1888, but the ASPCA lives on. The organization strives to abolish animal suffering through its many programs: education, adoption, rescue, poison control, and passing humane laws. In 2006, the ASPCA arrested more than 100 people for animal cruelty, found homes for 2,253 dogs and cats, and treated 24,120 animals at its hospitals. A year later, the organization awarded $365,000 in grants to equine organizations, proving that dogs and cats may have become the organization's mainstay, but Henry Bergh's ASPCA remains dedicated to the horses who inspired it.

*   *   *

The Great Crusader

Animals weren't Henry Bergh's only cause, and his reputation as a person who saved mistreated creatures put him at the forefront of the United States' first major child abuse case. Mary Ellen Wilson was a nine-year-old girl who had bounced from home to home until she ended up with Mary and Francis Connolly, a New York City couple who abused her. In 1874, Methodist missionary Etta Wheeler heard about the little girl's situation and contacted Bergh for help.

Bergh got in touch with the *New York Times*, which then ran a series of articles outlining Mary Ellen's plight. Bergh also sent one of the ASPCA's attorneys to petition for the child's removal from the Connollys' home. The judge granted the petition, and Mary Ellen eventually went to live with Etta Wheeler's family. Mary Connolly was found guilty of felonious assault and sent to prison. And the public outcry over the case led to the formation of the New York Society for the Prevention of Cruelty to Children.

The Original Mistys

*Just a few hours from the nation's capital, on an
island that straddles the Maryland/Virginia
border, a herd of horses roams free.*

Off the coast of Maryland and Virginia is Assateague, a
barrier island that's been home to a population of
wild horses for more than 300 years. The animals are often
called ponies, even though they're actually horses whose
size has been stunted because of their diet—salty marsh
grass and a lot of water, which also makes them look more
bloated than their relatives. But regardless of whether
they're horses or ponies, the black, white, brown, and
spotted animals have made the island famous.

Tax Evasion—17th-Century Style

There are several theories about how the horses got to
Assateague:

- Local folklore claims that a 16th-century Spanish
  galleon carrying a cargo of horses sank off the Virginia
  coast, and the horses who survived the wreck swam to
  shore.

- Other people think early colonists or pirates brought
  horses to the island.

- But most historians agree that the horses' ancestors

were probably abandoned on the island in the late 17th century by mainland owners who didn't want to comply with new fencing laws . . . and were also trying to avoid paying taxes on their livestock.

Today, the approximately 300 wild horses who live on Assateague are divided into two main herds, separated by a fence that cuts the island in half at the border between Maryland and Virginia.

Pony Penning

Every July, the Virginia herd is rounded up in an event called "pony penning," a practice that dates back hundreds of years. Originally, farmers and ranchers penned horses, sheep, and other livestock to

claim loose herds. Over the years, it became a social event: the farmers would pen the animals, and then the community would drink, eat, and celebrate together.

In 1924, the Chincoteague Volunteer Fire Department—headquartered just across the bay from Assateague Island in Chincoteague, Virginia—added a pony swim and auction to the penning festival in an effort to attract tourists (and money) to the area. On the day of the festival, volunteers round up the Virginia ponies (the ones on the Maryland side aren't included) and coax them to swim across the Assateague Channel to nearby Chincoteague. The "wild pony swim," which was mentioned in Marguerite Henry's novel *Misty of Chincoteague*, is a short swim of five to ten minutes and takes place at low tide for the safety of the spring foals.

While they're in Chincoteague, the horses are corralled for a few days to give visitors and residents a chance to admire them. Some of the horses are also auctioned off, in part to keep the size of the herd manageable. All of the money raised goes to the fire department. Two days after the auction, the remaining horses are herded back across the channel to the Virginia side of Assateague.

Don't Feed the Animals

Meanwhile, on the Maryland side, Assateague Island is a national seashore, protected and run by the National Park Service. Visitors can see the horses running or grazing along the shoreline, but there are strict no-feeding, no-petting rules. Beautiful as they are, the horses have been known to bite, kick, and charge after park visitors who don't keep a safe distance. So if you go, it's best to admire them from afar.

For more wild horses, turn to pages 116 and 129.

Lessons Learned

Horses show up in proverbs from around the world.

It is not the horse that draws the cart, but the oats.

—Russia

When you go to a donkey's house, don't talk about ears.

—Jamaica

Judge not the horse by his saddle.

—China

It is not enough for a man to know how to ride; he must know how to fall.

—Mexico

The wagon rests in winter, the sleigh in summer, the horse never.

—Yiddish

If three people say you are an ass, put on a bridle.

—Spain

In buying a horse or taking a wife, shut your eyes tight and commend yourself to God.

—Tuscany

Mighty Mustangs

Few things embody the romanticism of the
Wild West better than the mustang.

The word "mustang" comes from the Spanish *mesteño*, meaning "stray." Today, these equine strays roam in 10 Western states. Modern mustangs are descended from Spanish stock that escaped during the 17th and 18th centuries, and from horses who were brought west by ranchers. On the Plains, ranchers often released their horses in the winter and then recaptured them (or others) in the spring. Some never came home, and others became the property of the Native American tribes that raided European settlements. By the 1700s, mustangs were a staple among Native Americans in the West.

Catch and Release

In the 1830s, a smallpox epidemic swept through the Plains tribes. Unable to care for all their animals, the Native Americans released many of their mustangs into the wild. About 50 years later, when the U.S. government was trying to turn the tribes into farmers, officials introduced draft horses to some mustang herds to change the horse stock from a wild to a farming breed. As a result, different herds of modern mustangs can vary widely in appearance.

21

Mustangs can be any color, and they're strong and fast . . . often faster than domesticated horses. Catching them was tricky, and early ranchers and Native Americans used a process called "mustanging" to do it—lassoing the horses at a full gallop. (Among the Sioux, a lasso even became the symbol for a wild horse.) The fastest mustangs could easily escape a rider, so usually only the oldest and weakest horses were caught. In the early 1900s, though, cowboys started using motor vehicles, which made mustanging easier.

Free Again

Mustanging went on until 1971, when the U.S. Congress passed the Wild Free-Roaming Horse and Burro Act. The law made it illegal for a private citizen to capture or kill a mustang. (Government agencies do occasionally capture some of the horses to thin herds.) That brought the practice of mustanging to an end, and today, about 41,000 mustangs live in states from Arizona to Oregon, most in Nevada.

* * *

Good to Know

There are no albino horses. Why? Because the albino gene is fatal in horses.

Lost Breeds, Part 1

*The National Wildlife Federation estimates that 100 different animal
species become extinct every day. The* Equus *genus has lost
17 breeds that scientists know of. Here are three.*

The Ferghana

This breed was originally from Bactria (the northwestern
portion of ancient Afghanistan and Tajikistan) but was
named for the Ferghana region of central Asia. The
Ferghana ranged in color from mottled-white to peach and
red; had a long, flowing tail; and could travel as many as
300 miles a day. They also had two distinct bloodlines:

- **The hotbloods** resembled modern Arabians and had a
  long, narrow head, flaring nostrils, and a light gait.

- **The coldbloods** had bristly manes that were usually
  cropped, thick necks, and Roman-style noses.

China's second-century emperor Wu-ti especially loved
Ferghana horses and wanted to bring them east. When the
rulers of Bactria objected, Wu-ti invaded and defeated them,
and then proceeded to take all the horses he wanted. One
hundred of Bactria's finest breeding stock plus 3,000 other
horses were shipped off to China, thus beginning the era of
the country's "sweating blood" horses—so named because
the Chinese thought they actually sweated blood.

(Historians think that blood-sucking parasites bit the Ferghana horses as they worked, causing the animals to look like they sweated blood.) Soon these horses became the favored mount of the military and the Imperial Court, and statues of the Ferghana appeared in all types of Chinese art.

Eventually, Ferghana horses arrived in the Middle East by way of the Moors, who took them to Spain. They came to North America in the 1500s via an expedition into northern Arizona. By the 1800s, escaped Ferghanas were running wild all over the West, but over the next 100 years, because of excessive crossbreeding worldwide, the distinctive Ferghana disappeared.

The Turkoman

The most remarkable quality of the Turkoman breed—originally from the area that's now Turkmenistan—was its stamina. These horses could travel 900 miles in 11 consecutive days, drinking water only every three days and eating sparse desert grass. That hardiness made them extremely valuable to early populations in this arid region.

Turkoman horses looked a lot like modern Arabians—slender with lean bodies, small muzzles, and long necks and backs. They stood 15 to 16 hands tall and had generally solid coats of white, gray, or black. The Turkomans had almost no mane, and their coats glistened with a silky metallic glow. Bred and raised on the central Asian steppes, these horses were extremely fast—they could easily outrun and outlast any of the predators of that region

. . . and they were equally adept in the water. No one knows exactly when the breed became extinct. They were around until at least the early 17th century, and there are records of them racing on English tracks. By about 1625, though, they were gone.

The Narragansett Pacer

There's some disagreement about where the Narragansett pacer came from. Some researchers say the breed was a result of crossing the Irish hobby and the Scottish Galloway pony, but others say the Narragansett came from the Spanish Jennet's bloodline. Either way, the horse was developed in Rhode Island in the 17th century.

Narragansett pacers were small—about 14 hands tall, on average—and, by many accounts, ugly. They were generally sorrel-colored with a spray of white markings and had unusually long necks. But they were fast and could reportedly travel a mile in less than two minutes.

The American colonists used them as racehorses. But even though the animals were considered equine aristocrats in the colonies, breeders didn't like their homely appearance. So the colonists carefully selected and bred Narragansetts with the best, fastest, and most handsome English pacers, giving rise to the modern standardbred. By the end of the Revolutionary War, the breed was extinct.

For two more lost breeds, turn to page 92.

Cowboy Jokes

*Herding, roping, branding . . . how did cowboys
find the time to come up with such great jokes?*

The Horse Knows

One day while he was building a barn, the cowboy lost
his favorite book. A week later, one of his horses came up
to him holding the book in its mouth. The cowboy was
stunned. He took the book from the horse and said, "It's a
miracle!"

"Not exactly," said the horse. "Your name is written
inside."

Sink or Swim

Back in the Wild West, three cowboys
were about to be hanged for stealing
cattle. The lynch mob brought them
to the bank of a nearby river
and planned to string them up
from a branch over the water. That
way, when the men died, they'd just
drop into the river and float away.
The mob put the noose around the first
cowboy's neck, but he was so sweaty

that he slipped right out, fell into the water, and swam away. When the mob strung up the second cowboy, he also slipped out of the noose and got away. As they pulled the third man toward the noose, he was hesitant, and said "Hey! Would you tighten that noose? I can't swim!"

* * *

The Cowboy Creed

1. Don't squat with your spurs on.

2. Don't interfere with something that isn't bothering you.

3. If you find yourself in a hole, stop digging.

4. Never drink downstream from the herd.

5. Telling a man to get lost and making him do it are two different things.

6. When you give an animal a lesson in meanness, don't be surprised if he learns the lesson.

7. When you ride ahead of the herd, look back once in a while to make sure it's still there.

8. Easiest way to double your money: fold it in two and put it in your pocket.

9. If you start feeling like you're a man with some influence, try ordering around another man's horse.

10. Never miss the opportunity to keep your mouth shut.

And They're Off!

On May 17, 1875, in front of a crowd of about 10,000 people, 15 three-year-old horses competed in the first Kentucky Derby. In the years since, this first leg of the Triple Crown has become "the most exciting two minutes in sports" and is America's oldest continuously held sporting event.

Nickname: "The Run for the Roses," for the blanket of 554 roses draped over the winner

Racetrack: Churchill Downs, named after John and Henry Churchill, who provided the land for the racetrack. The Churchills were relatives of Meriwether Lewis Clark Jr. (grandson of explorer William Clark), who founded the Louisville Jockey Club.

Date: First Saturday in May
Course: 1¼ miles, dirt track
Field: 3-year-old Thoroughbreds
Purse: $2 million (2008)

Notable Jockeys

- Between 1875 and 1902, African American jockeys won 15 of the 28 Derbys. Thirteen out of 14 starters in the first Derby were African Americans, and one,

Oliver Lewis, rode Aristides to victory in the first Derby race. (They placed second in the Belmont Stakes.)

- The youngest rider to win a Derby was 15-year-old African American jockey Alonzo Clayton, in 1892.
- Eddie Arcaro and Bill Hardtack are tied for the most Derby wins: five each.

Traditions

- The mint julep—a drink consisting of bourbon, mint, sugar, and crushed ice—is the traditional beverage. And burgoo, a thick stew typically made with lamb (sometimes with beef, chicken, or pork) and vegetables, is also served.
- The University of Louisville marching band plays Stephen Foster's "My Old Kentucky Home" during the horses' post parade in front of the grandstands.
- The Kentucky governor awards the rose garland and trophy to the winner.

Milestones

1915: Regret was the first filly to win the Derby. Only two others have matched that feat: Genuine Risk (1980) and Winning Colors (1988).

1917: English-bred Omar Khayyam was the first foreign-bred horse to win.

1952: First national television coverage of the Kentucky Derby.

1954: The purse exceeded $100,000 for the first time.

1968: The first and only time a horse has won the race and been disqualified. Dancer's Image was stripped of his title after traces of a banned substance were found in his urine. The drug in question—phenylbutazone—was later legalized for use by racehorses in many states, including Kentucky.

1970: Diane Crump became the first female jockey to ride in the Derby.

1973: Secretariat crossed the finish line with the fastest time ever run in the Derby (at its present distance) at 1:59.4. The record still stands.

2005: The purse distribution was changed so that horses finishing fifth would get a share; previously, only the first four finishers received any.

* * *

That's a Record
The Derby is restricted to three-year-olds, and only one horse has won it without racing at age two: Apollo in 1882.

Hay Is for Horses

*From scrub brush to sugar beets, horse
feed has come a long, long way.*

An Evolving Diet

Ancient people from Greece, Rome, and Egypt held horses
in high esteem, both because of the animals' prominent
role in mythology and because only wealthy citizens could
afford them. Horses in those days grazed on native grasses
and shrubs . . . and just about any other vegetation they
could find in their free-ranging paths. Alexander the
Great is said to have augmented his horses' diet with
oats—a luxury that, at the time, only a royal could afford.

Explorers brought horses to the Americas as early as
the 1500s, and those colonial workhorses ate wild grass
and brush during warm months and whatever scraps
their owners could provide in the winter. Since food was
scarce, colonists were often forced to turn their horses
loose because they couldn't afford to feed them through
the lean seasons.

It's Supplemental

When American colonists began to prosper, though,
their animals also fared better. By the 18th and 19th
centuries, settlers were supplementing their horses' diet

of wild grass and hay with boiled barley and other grains. In 1834, British entrepreneur Thomas Day introduced the first dietary supplement for horses, known as the "Black Drink." No one knows exactly what was in the mysterious bottles, but horses loved it and horse owners bought it in droves.

By the early 20th century, horse owners were helping their animals digest all the roughage in their grass-and-hay diets with a little cod liver oil. In 1935, a formula designed especially for horses, called Super Solvitax Pure Cod Liver Oil, appeared in tack and feed shops. By the 1950s, horse diets included numerous concentrated supplements (in the form of pellets, cubes, and dry mixes): high-carbohydrate grains for extra energy, linseed for protein, and herbs for additional vitamins and minerals.

Modern-Day Grub

The well-fed horse today continues to enjoy a diet of mostly hay, and now there is a wide range of designer hays bred to be especially nutritious—like Lucerne Farm's special blend of timothy, oat, and alfalfa hays and Aden Brook Farm's bales of pure alfalfa.

There are also even more supplement choices to provide horses with additional calories and nutrients. In addition to good old carrots and apples for energy and added fiber, sugar-beet pulp aids digestion, and salt licks maintain proper sodium balance. (Horse owners beware: All salt licks are not created equal. They are formulated with trace minerals, so it is important to offer your horse a salt lick designed for equines.)

In addition, concentrated grain supplements enriched with vitamins, minerals, and specially formulated antioxidants are widely used. And because of the worry that pellet forms of these concentrates could contain unwanted material, many horse owners prefer to feed their horses these complex grains in a loose form, coated in a sticky syrup that makes the mixture more palatable.

Not Good Eats

There are some things horses should never be allowed to eat: milkweed, elderberry, and oleander, because they are all poisonous. Pokeweed, azaleas, and mesquite can cause diarrhea and intestinal discomfort. And black walnuts can lead to depression and colic in horses.

*   *   *

Women didn't start riding sidesaddle until the 15th century.

The Horse Lingo
IQ Test

Solve this quiz using terms that only a horse lover would know.

1. If your horse is "bomb proof," what doesn't he do?

2. How many flakes are in a bale?

3. Cowboys use piggin' strings to tie the legs of what animals?

4. Monkey nose taps protect a rider's what?

5. When a Thoroughbred "breaks his maiden," he's just done what?

6. A skewbald is a pinto that does not have spots of what color?

7. If a horseman owns a fast mare, a faster gelding, and an even faster stallion, which one will win a distaff race?

8. If a horse is a "hard keeper," what does he have trouble maintaining?

9. What do "rough string" horses do when they are saddled?

10. What does it mean if a horse has been "roached"?

Answers on page 222.

The History of Horseshoes

A lot like human shoes (though definitely less stylish), horseshoes have been protecting feet for centuries.

Sandal Up!

The inventor of the horseshoe is lost to history, but the idea has been around for a long time. Asian horsemen from the second century BC put booties made from hides or plants on their horses' feet to protect them from injury. And sometime after the first century AD, the Romans introduced leather and metal "hipposandals," which attached to a horse's hooves with leather straps.

Over the next few hundred years, there were some references in literature to horseshoes—in particular, a Koran from the seventh century talks about cavalry horses that "strike fire by dashing their hoofs against the stone." But it wasn't until 910 that the horseshoe showed up definitively in print: Byzantine emperor Leo VI mentioned horses' "crescent-figured irons and their nails." By about 1000, metal horseshoes were common in Europe and Asia.

Ruling with an Iron Shoe

One of the reasons for the shoes' popularity was that iron had become cheaper and more plentiful by the 11th century. Also, soldiers heading off on the Crusades liked large

Flemish horses, but the animals had flat, weak feet (because they lived mostly in damp areas). So horseshoes were necessary to protect their sensitive hooves. In fact, horseshoes became such an important commodity that, in some places, they could be used as money. Horseshoes remained mostly a military accessory, though, until the 13th and 14th centuries, when improvements in manufacturing meant that shoes could be mass-produced and bought ready-made.

Horseshoes on the Rise

By the 1600s in Europe, horseshoeing was a full-fledged business. Back then, farriers in Great Britain and France were also horse doctors. During the 17th century, though, they stopped practicing equine medicine and became full-time blacksmiths.

With the onset of the Industrial Revolution, horseshoe use and production grew even more. The first machine to cast shoes en masse appeared in 1800, but the first patent for a horseshoe-manufacturing machine was issued in 1835 to New Yorker Henry Burden, who could make 60 shoes every hour. In the 1860s, the Union army had its own machine to make horseshoes, an invaluable tool that gave their cavalries an advantage over the South during the Civil War.

Little has changed in the horseshoe's basic design since then. Farriers still use the U-shape horseshoes that they nail (or sometimes glue) onto the horse's hoof. Steel and aluminum are the most common metals used, but shoes can also incorporate rubber, plastic, magnesium, titanium, and copper. Sports like jumping, eventing, and polo require strong, durable shoes made from steel, but racehorses need light feet, so aluminum is the preferred metal for the track.

Barefooting

Not everyone thinks horses need shoes, though. In the wild, of course, horses go barefoot and mostly do fine— natural wear helps to toughen and trim their hooves. And just because shoeing has a long history and has become the most mainstream method of hoof care, say the anti-horseshoers, there's no reason not to strive for a more natural lifestyle.

Officially called the "barefoot horse movement," supporters of this cause have been around for decades and argue that when horses' feet are trimmed and cared for properly, they don't need shoes. The type of terrain the horse trains on is the most important factor. And besides being more comfortable for the horse, the benefits of going natural include a lower risk of laminitis and navicular syndrome, both of which can make horses lame and, in some cases, can threaten their lives.

Going from shod to barefoot can be a long process, and horses have to spend at least a year training on natural surfaces like grass and dirt before they develop tough enough feet to walk on hard surfaces like cement and asphalt. But once their feet adapt, they can go almost anywhere shod horses can. (Hoof boots can provide protection during the transition.)

*   *   *

Hoofed Golden Retrievers?

Gypsy horses are docile and sturdy, qualities that have earned them the nickname "golden retrievers with hooves." About 100 years ago, nomadic Roma gypsies in England and Ireland started breeding these horses specifically for that temperament. The Roma needed low-maintenance draft horses to pull their wagons. And they wanted their horses to reflect their peaceful culture. Aggressive horses were usually sold to maintain the breed's friendly nature.

Today, gypsy horses go by several names: Irish cobs, Irish tinkers, gypsy cobs, and others. But they're all the same, sturdy draft horses, recognizable by their silky tails and manes, feathered legs, hardiness, and gentle disposition.

Big Red²

Man o' War or Secretariat? When it came to picking the greatest racehorse of all time, we just couldn't choose a favorite.

Man o' War

The Early Years: In 1917, Eleanor Belmont (wife of August Belmont Jr. of the Belmont Stakes) named her stable's new foal Man o' War to honor her husband's service in World War I. (Actually, she tried to name the horse "My Man o' War," but when she sent in his registration to the Jockey Club, they dropped "My" from the name.)

Soon after, the Belmonts had to sell their yearlings—the war years were tough financially—and horseman Sam Ridder bought the colt for $5,000. (Later, Ridder turned down $1 million for Man o' War.) The fiery, chestnut colt was difficult to break, and when a jockey mounted Man o' War for the first time, the horse threw him 40 feet.

Life at the Track: In 1919, in his first race at Belmont Park, "Big Red" (so nicknamed because of his color) won by six lengths. Three days later, he won the Keene Memorial Stakes. Then, despite carrying 130 pounds of extra weight as a handicap, the two-year old easily took his next four races. Soon, racing pundits claimed that Big Red was unbeatable.

In the two seasons he competed, Man o' War ran in 21 races—and won 20 times. The one time he missed out on the winner's circle, he came in second. An error on the part of the starter caused him to enter the race late, and his flustered jockey let them get boxed in so that Man o' War couldn't race to the lead. Stable employees claimed that Big Red had nightmares after the defeat. In fact, what made the big horse so endearing to many fans was the contrast between his bold winning ways and his anxious demeanor between races. In the barn while waiting to race, Man o' War nervously chewed on his hooves like a person chewing on fingernails—especially if he couldn't spend time with his beloved stable companion, a horse named Major Treat.

Big Wins: During his career, Man o' War set three world records, two American records, and three track records. He was such a star that the Jockey Club handicapper wanted to put more weight on him than any horse had ever carried. But rather than risk injury, Ridder retired Man o' War to a stud farm where he lived until his death in 1947. Many racing buffs consider Man o' War the greatest of all racehorses, and on *Blood-Horse* magazine's list of the 100 best racehorses of the 20th century, Man o' War is first.

Secretariat
The Early Years: But what about Secretariat? Sure, he ranks #2 on *Blood-Horse*'s list, but he also has quite a

record. In 1969, breeder Penny Cherney lost a coin toss. The winner, Ogden Phipps, got to choose the foal he wanted from the mating of his stallion Bold Ruler and Cherney's mare, Somethingroyal. Phipps chose the first foal the pair produced, leaving Cherney with the second— a chestnut colt named Secretariat, who was born on March 29, 1970.

Life at the Track: Like Man o' War, Secretariat was big and red. But unlike Man o' War, young Secretariat didn't win his first race. That contest began with a traffic jam at the starting gate—the colt nearly fell, but managed to finish fourth. Secretariat won his next races easily, though, and by the time his first season was over, the new "Big Red" had won the Hopeful Stakes, the Belmont Futurity, the Laurel Futurity, and the Garden State Stakes, among others. He was so impressive on the track that polls named him Horse of the Year—a rare honor for a two-year-old.

Big Wins: In 1973, just his second racing season, three-year-old Secretariat won the Kentucky Derby in 1:59.4 seconds, a record that still stands today. He then won the Preakness. It had been 25 years since Citation had won the Triple Crown, but after the Derby and the Preakness, the media, public, and racing aficionados believed that Secretariat would be the next one to do it.

Finally, on June 9, 1973, before an audience of more than 60,000 in the stands, Secretariat ran what many people say was the greatest race of all time. He won the Belmont Stakes by 31 lengths (about 240 feet), and his time of 2:24 for 1½ miles set a world record that has yet to be broken. The week after the race, Secretariat was on the cover of *Time*, *Newsweek*, and *Sports Illustrated*. Today, he's still ranked among the top 100 athletes (human or otherwise) of the 20th century.

To read about more famous racehorses,
turn to page 58 and 145.

*　　*　　*

Silly as It Seems

Incitatus may have been the most pampered horse in history—if only by a madman. The ancient Roman emperor Caligula loved horse racing, and the white stallion Incitatus was his favorite steed. Caligula appointed 18 servants to tend to the horse's needs, and Incitatus lived in a marble and ivory stable. Oats with gold flakes were his regular fare, and he often wore clothes and jewels to official banquets held in his honor.

Don't Forget Your Corset

Horses were a vital part of American history, so it's no surprise that there are some looney laws about them. Some of these are still on the books.

Maryland: It's illegal for a horse to sleep in a bathtub unless his owner sleeps with him.

Georgia: Horses can't "neigh" after 10:00 pm.

Washington: It's illegal to ride an ugly horse.

Nebraska: A man can't ride on horseback without his wife until the couple has been married for one year.

New Jersey: It's illegal to pass a horse-drawn carriage on the street.

California: Horses can't mate within 500 yards of a church, school, or tavern.

North Dakota: Every house within the city limits of Bismarck has to have a hitching post.

Virginia: Married women who ride horses through the town of Upperville while wearing "body hugging clothing" can be fined up to $2.

Ohio: Men may not "make remarks to or concerning, or cough, or whistle at, or do any other act to attract the attention of any woman riding a horse."

Iowa: It's illegal for horses to eat fire hydrants.

Louisiana: Horses cannot be tied to trees on public highways.

New York: It's illegal to open or close an umbrella when a horse is around.

Tennessee: In Cumberland County, the horse speed limit is 3 mph.

Texas: No one can take pictures of horses on Sunday. (The fine for doing so is $1.50.)

New Mexico: Women who ride horses in public have to wear corsets.

Arizona: Cowboys may not walk through the lobby of a hotel with their spurs on.

Great Horses in Small Packages

*Here's a look at some little horses who
inspire big love in a lot of people.*

A Mini History

Miniature horses have been around for centuries—their
remains have even been found in the tombs of Egyptian
pharaohs. But the first known miniature horse breeding program began about 400 years ago with the royal Hapsburg
family. A short time later, the horses showed up as an
attraction at the Versailles palace zoo in France. And in the
mid-1800s, the French empress Eugenie used miniature
horses to pull her carriage.

But when the nobility in France and other parts of
Europe fell on hard times because of peasant uprisings and
rebellions, the royals didn't have the money to maintain
their tiny horses' cushy lifestyle. The horses were mostly
sold as pets, but some went to European traveling circuses,
where the animals learned to do tricks. They also worked
in coal mines, pulled peat carts, and plowed fields. And a
handful of minihorse lovers kept refining or producing
new breeds of small horses.

The Big Mini Comeback

By the 20th century, most of the world had forgotten about miniature horses. But that changed in 1962 when an Argentinean breeder, Juan Falabella, sold three of his rare Falabella horses (which resemble mini-Thoroughbred/Arabian horses) to President John F. Kennedy, who gave them as Christmas presents to his children. Soon photos of the little Falabellas grazing on the White House lawn appeared on the covers of news magazines, and interest in owning mini horses skyrocketed.

Today, miniature horses are one of the fastest-growing types. The American Miniature Horse Association (AMHA)—the leading miniature horse registry—lists about 160,000 of them worldwide.

But What Makes a Miniature Horse?

They come in nearly all colors—though not all sizes. Full-grown miniature horses must be no higher than 34 inches at the withers. Despite their small size, though, they aren't considered ponies because minis still have many horse characteristics: thinner manes and tails, lighter bones, and proportionally larger heads than ponies. A typical mini eats about a half a flake of hay (1½ pounds) and a cup of grain each day. They weigh 250 pounds or less and usually live into their 30s, though some have reached more than 50 years of age. As a breed, minis are friendly, gentle, and intelligent.

They can have genetic problems, though. Most mini horse registries (including the AMHA) try to improve the lives of miniature horses by working to eliminate dwarfism from bloodlines. Although all mini horses possess some of the genetic markers for dwarfism, some breeders used to deliberately breed dwarfs to get the smallest horses possible. The practice is now discouraged because the dwarf gene causes painful deformities that cripple and even kill miniature horses. Seventeen-inch Thumbelina (officially, the world's smallest horse) is a dwarf who only comes up to the shins of standard minis. Because her legs are proportionally smaller than her body and her head, she has to wear orthopedic fittings to strengthen her limbs.

Minis to the Rescue

Mini horses take on many of the same jobs and functions their larger cousins do. They make great pets, of course, and also compete in miniature horse shows where winners take home trophies and sometimes thousands of dollars. Minis are too small to be ridden by adults, so the owner usually walks alongside the horse. In a performance-class competition, people might run beside their horses while the minis jump small obstacles, or an owner might drive a cart pulled by the horse.

Some minis even work as service animals. In 2003, the Texas Veterinary Medical Association inducted Buttons, an eight-year-old miniature stallion, into the Texas Animal Hall of Fame "because of the happiness he brings by visiting local nursing home residents and handicapped children in north Texas." At 32½ inches tall, Buttons is small enough to walk right into the rooms of patients to cheer them up. In one case, an elderly woman who had refused to speak hugged Buttons, cried, and spoke enthusiastically about her love for horses.

Pint-Sized Help

Other minis act as seeing-eye horses for the blind. Cuddles, a seeing-eye horse from Ellsworth, Maine, wears leather sneakers to keep her from slipping on floors inside buildings. It's all in a day's work for the 24-inch-tall, 55-pound mini who guides her blind owner.

And Rosie from Arizona visits schools for children with disabilities. The children, who might be intimidated by the size of a large horse, eagerly embrace Rosie. Properly trained, mini horses can help children with disabilities to stand and walk—they can even pull wheelchairs. Once the playthings of royalty, today's mini horses are working hard to make a big and positive impact on the world.

From Eohippus to Horse

Before there were horses, there was eohippus. Here's how the little prehistorian got its start on the long road to horsehood.

Rhino Relatives

Eohippus lived about 50 to 60 million years ago in the Northern Hemisphere and is believed to be the ancestor of modern horses, rhinos, and piglike mammals called tapirs. It was just two feet long and eight or nine inches high at the shoulder—about the size of a small dog. It had four hoofed toes on its front feet, three hoofed toes on each hind foot, a long skull, and 44 teeth.

Eohippus didn't look like a horse at all. It had short legs, a short neck, pads on its toes, and an arched back. The animal made its home in European and North American forests, where its diet consisted mostly of leaves. Over time, though, the Earth's forests started to shrink, and grasslands spread. So eohippus wandered out into the open and started to nibble on grass.

Evolving Eohippus

Plants have to evolve to survive, too, though, so over the next few million years, some of them developed strategies to prevent them from being eaten. In particular, one of eohippus's main food sources, the "lallang" grasses, developed jagged grains of sand called *silica* in their leaves. That wore down the eohippus' teeth, so some of the horses died off. The ones who had bigger teeth with thicker enamel lived long enough to reproduce. In turn, their offspring developed longer faces with stronger jaws to make even better use of those big, strong teeth.

But while the horses were out there out on the wide-open grasslands, they were easy pickings for predators. So the animals had to be speedy to survive. New generations were longer-legged, faster, stronger, and had fewer toes, until they evolved into the look and size of modern horses.

Dig It

In 1841, an English paleontologist named Richard Owen found the first evidence of eohippus: a tooth and part of a jawbone. He suspected it was a horse ancestor because of the tooth, but others initially thought the fossils belonged to a monkey and concluded (incorrectly) that England must have once been a jungle. Over time, though, other scientists figured out that they didn't come from monkeys at all, but from small horses.

Then, in 1867, American paleontologists dug up the first complete eohippus skeleton in western Wyoming. A few years later, scientist Othniel C. Marsh named the creature *eohippus* (or "dawn horse"). The Wyoming find finally revealed a true picture of the horse's earliest relative.

Take a Cab, Not a Horse

Drunks can cause a lot of chaos when they're horsing around.

But He Stops at Red Lights!

In June 2005, Millard G. Dwyer—a man from Kentucky with a history of DUIs in vehicles and on horseback—was caught riding his horse drunk again. This brought Dwyer's total number of incidents involving both alcohol and horses to three . . . in less than two months. This time, he was weaving around the road, holding up a long line of traffic, and nearly falling off his Tennessee walking horse, Prince. Lieutenant Allan Coomer said, "Usually after the first arrest a lot of them will learn, but this guy was back out there again."

Dwyer, however, argued that his horse was accustomed to walking along roads and could carry him home safely without guidance—the horse even knew to stop at red lights. "He said that the horse had a mind of its own and had been in complete control of the situation," Coomer recalled.

Fall-Down Drunk

One night in 2007, in Culpepper, Virginia, Eric Scott Kyff and Lauren J. Allen—both drunk and on horseback—stopped at a 7–11 store. The pair captured the attention of off-duty police officers (and bystanders) when Kyff urinated outside the store. When the onlookers protested, Kyff angrily mounted his horse and tried to run them over. He and Allen eventually fled on their horses, but police cars were already on the way. A chase ensued, with cop cars chasing the suspects on horseback. But Allen soon fell of her horse, and Kyff was thrown off when he ran into a utility wire. The two faced charges of public intoxication, obstruction of justice, and riding on a highway after dark without proper reflective material.

The kicker: This was the duo's second arrest that year for saddling up while intoxicated. The first time, they wanted to ride their horses home to avoid driving when two officers confronted them. Both horses and humans were held overnight—the humans in jail and the horses in front of the police station across the street.

Using Beauty as a Battering Ram

Melissa Byrum York was arrested in 2007 after police received an unusual report: The intoxicated woman was riding her horse at midnight on the streets of Sylvania, Alabama. "Cars were passing by having to avoid it, and almost hitting the horse," said Police Chief Brad Gregg. When Officer John Seals attempted to stop York, she refused to dismount. Instead, she used her horse to batter Seals's police car. York then tried to flee on foot but got her shoe twisted up in the stirrup, leaving her attached to her horse, where she was easily arrested.

York was charged with seven counts, including DUI, resisting arrest, assault, attempting to elude police, and animal cruelty. (At least one charge—assault—was dropped after authorities decided a horse could not be considered a deadly weapon.) Gregg reported, "From what I've heard, the horse was in pretty rough shape after all this . . . [York] was pretty hard on the horse." Luckily, there was a safe place nearby for the animal to stay. Deputy Brian Keck owned a pasture and took custody of the horse for its protection.

* * *

Horse Talk

"Be wary of the horse with a sense of humor"
> —*Pam Brown, writer*

"Horses and children, I often think, have a lot of the good sense there is in the world."
> —*Josephine Demott Robinson, circus performer*

The Name Game

When it comes time to name your horse,
choosing the right one can be tricky.

Registration Tips

If you want to register your horse's name, you'll need to get all the rules from the breed's registry. Some breeds require that you use part of the sire and dam's names. Others, like Austrias' Haflinger, have to start with a particular letter. And most limit the number of letters. Be sure to submit several possibilities because most registries don't allow duplicate names. (The registry will make the final choice.)

Get Creative

Many people like to choose something unique for their horse's name. That's where the "Horse Name Generator" at ultimatehorsesite.com comes in. The site claims to have more than one million possibilities. Here are a few fun ones:

Frosted Gold   Anaconda Pirate
Tinted Whiskey   Photosynthetic
Mighty Serenade   Gingerbread
Blotched Doughnut   Flame-Throwing
Doodle Implosion   Conclusion

Horse Myths

Since antiquity, horses have fired the human imagination.
Here are two horselike creatures from ancient Greece.

From the Centaur of the Earth

The legend of the centaur—a creature with the body of a
horse and the torso of a man—probably arose when cultures that did not ride horses were invaded by warriors
who did. From afar, the horse and rider might have looked
like a half-man/half-horse monster, and over time, people
created myths to explain them.

According to the ancient Greeks, centaurs were a powerful race of beings who served one of two functions: some
were teachers, but others were followers of Dionysus, the
god of wine. As such, many of them were fond of drinking
and debauchery. (Their penchant for kidnapping maidens
represented man's bestial and violent nature.)

The centaurs' origins are murky. They were descended
from Ixion, who tricked and killed his father-in-law.
Because his crime was so heinous, none of the gods would
allow him to atone for his evil deed.

Zeus took pity on him, though, and invited him to
dinner on Mt. Olympus—where the ungrateful dinner
guest immediately set about seducing Hera, Zeus's wife.
When the king of the gods got wind of the plan, he made

a double of Hera out of clouds. According to some stories, the fruits of the relationship between Ixion and the cloud were the centaurs. Other legends claim that the centaurs were actually the grandchildren of the pair. Either way, one (Chiron) was different from the rest. Chiron was a wise and skilled medicine man who served as a tutor to many of the Greek mythical heroes. Chiron was also immortal, but when he was accidentally wounded by a poisoned arrow, he suffered so much from the wound that he gave away his immortality to a god named Prometheus (best known for bringing fire to mankind). Chiron was then able to die peacefully, and his descendants were the wise, academic centaurs.

Modern Myth: The centaur character has appeared in everything from the Harry Potter and Lord of the Rings series to John Updike's 1964 National Book Award winner, *The Centaur*. NASA even named its high-energy rocket *Centaur*. The rocket sends communication satellites into space and is referred to as "America's Workhorse in Space."

Pegasus of My Heart

The winged horse Pegasus was the son of the sea god Poseidon and the snake-haired monster Medusa. He (and his twin brother, the giant Chrysaor) sprang from Medusa's neck when a hero named Perseus severed her head. (In another version of the same story, Pegasus and Chrysaor sprang from the drops of blood that dripped onto the ground from Medusa's severed head.)

Using a golden bridle that Athena, the goddess of war, had given him, Greek hero Bellerophon captured and tamed Pegasus. Together, hero and horse set about conquering the world. At this point, though, Bellerophon got too big for his britches—he tried to scale Mt. Olympus and live among the gods. Zeus was in no mood for uninvited guests, though, so he sent an insect to sting Pegasus. This caused the horse to rear and throw Bellerophon, who fell back to Earth to live out his days disabled and blind.

With Bellerophon out of the picture, Pegasus was welcomed into the gods' abode, where Eos, the goddess of dawn, claimed him. Pegasus was made into a constellation that bears his name, which appears in the spring sky.

Modern Myth: In modern culture, Pegasus is known as the symbol of Mobil gas and oil (Exxon Mobil Corp.) and the mascot of TriStar Pictures. And in England during World War II, the country's parachute forces used Bellerophon astride Pegasus as their insignia to symbolize warriors swooping into battle from above.

* * *

Sneaky, Sneaky

In computer lingo, a Trojan Horse is a program that messes up your hard drive. Unlike a computer virus that replicates, the Trojan horse hides in plain sight, waiting for you to think it's a useful program and execute it.

Off to the Races:
The Godolphin Arabian
and Eclipse

Horse races have thrilled spectators since 5000 BC, when the first nomads staged competitions across the steppes of central Asia. Here are two of the greatest horses to influence the sport and find their way into the history books.

The Godolphin Arabian: An Original Sire

Thoroughbred racing as we know it developed in the 17th and 18th centuries after Europeans discovered the speed and stamina of Bedouin horses during the Crusades. European nobility imported Arabian stallions to breed to their mares, and all of today's Thoroughbreds can trace their lineage back to three primary stallions from the Middle East: the Darley Arabian, Godolphin Arabian, and Byerley Turk. Perhaps the most famous of those is the Godolphin Arabian.

In 1724, a bay foal named Shami was born in Yemen. He was first presented to the Bey of Tunis (the Tunisian head of state) and then given to King Louis XV of France as a gift. But the French court considered the horse unsuitable for breeding—at just 14.3 hands, he was small, and the trip from Tunis was hard on him. He looked thin and had a dull coat, not what the French considered to be good stock. So in 1729, King Louis sold him to the English horse breeder Edward Cooke.

Cooke also considered Shami inferior, but bred him anyway . . . with the mare Lady Roxanne, who produced a foal named Lath. That horse became England's greatest racer of the day, winning the Queen's Plate race at Newmarket nine times. Suddenly, Shami was in demand for stud. The Earl of Godolphin bought him in 1733 and renamed him the Godolphin Arabian. Shami's foals not only dominated racing in the 18th century, they also became the sires and dams of champions. Even 20th-century track greats like Man o' War and Seabiscuit had pedigrees that led back to the small Arabian horse from Tunis.

Eclipse: The Horse from Nowhere

On April 1, 1764, two major events occurred: one was a solar eclipse, and the other was the birth of a colt named Eclipse (in honor of the astronomical event). Eclipse belonged to the English Duke of Cumberland, but when the duke died a year later, the horse was sold to William Wildman, a sheep dealer. Wildman may have worried that he got a bad deal—Eclipse was not only high-strung and hard to handle, the horse also galloped with his nose almost touching the ground.

Despite his problems, Eclipse entered his first race in 1769. It was a race of four separate heats, each a mile long. By the beginning of the second heat, spectator Captain Dennis O'Kelly was so impressed with Eclipse's stamina that he made one of the world's most daring (and now famous) bets. In those days, any horse lagging more than 240 yards behind the front-runner was said to be "nowhere." O'Kelly bet that the race would end with "Eclipse first, and the rest, nowhere." Eclipse won; his competitors were, in fact, nowhere, and the exuberant O'Kelly bought a half interest in the horse.

Eclipse went on to win every race he entered. He was so fast that after two years no one would bet on any other horse when Eclipse was in the lineup. So he was retired to stud, and today at least 80 percent of racing's Thoroughbreds (including Canada's Northern Dancer) are descendants of the great racehorse who left his competition "nowhere."

For Man o' War and Secretariat, turn to page 39.
To read about Citation and Ruffian, turn to page 145.

Perfume and Ponies

In 1947, a horse named Jet Pilot won the Kentucky Derby.
Most people don't remember him, but they do know
his owner: cosmetics queen Elizabeth Arden.

Queen of the Stable

Elizabeth Arden made her fortune in cosmetics, but by
1947, her name, her Kentucky stable (Maine Chance
Farm), and the cherry, blue, and white racing silks her
jockeys wore were well known in racing circles. In 1945,
the horses of Maine Chance won more money than any
other Thoroughbred stable in America, and in 1946,
Elizabeth Arden the racehorse owner made the cover of
Time magazine.

Arden's enthusiastic interest in horses was no accident.
Born in 1878 to a farm family near Toronto, Canada, the
young girl took responsibility for tending the family
horses. It was a long time before she had a horse of her
own, though. She grew up to make a fortune in the cosmetics industry and, in 1931, finally invested some of her
money in her first Thoroughbred—How High. Soon after,
her flamboyant styel set tongues wagging throughout racing circles.

Mrs. Mud Pack

The décor of Arden's stables mimicked that of her famous Red Door salons. Hanging plants adorned the horse stalls. Soothing music was piped into the barns. Arden was quoted as saying, "Treat a horse like a woman and a woman like a horse, and they'll both win for you."

She wasn't joking. According to biographer Lindy Woodhead, Arden's stable boys referred to her as "Mrs. Mud Pack." Her horses were regularly massaged with her Eight Hour Cream. Ardena Skin Tonic Lotion was used to wash them. She insisted that the stalls and jockey silks be scented with her Blue Grass perfume. And no matter where the horses were stabled—at home or at racetracks around the country—their diet included clover shipped from Maine.

Although she pampered her horses, Arden was tough on her stable staff and trainers. They either did things her way, or they were replaced. Over a 30-year period she hired and fired more than 60 trainers.

Suspicious Flame

In 1946, Arden's horses were at the pinnacle of Thoroughbred racing. Then in May, her barn at Illinois' Arlington Park racetrack caught fire. It was suspicious— the fire was isolated to her barn, two grooms who were supposed to be on duty through the night were mysteriously absent, and unlike every other barn at the track, Arden's was pitch dark. Arden's horses had begun to dominate racing. (She had three entered in that year's Kentucky Derby.) And rumors abounded that some of the unsavory characters involved in the industry—notably gamblers and organized crime figures—wanted to "put her in her place."

The fire's cause was never determined, and Arden lost 23 of the 28 horses she had quartered at Arlington. But she persevered, and Jet Pilot, who wasn't there for the fire, went on to win the Derby the next year.

It's Who You Know

One key to Arden's success in horseracing was her connection to the sport's high echelon. Her first winning horse, named Grand Union, was a grandson of the legendary Man o' War. It was Man o' War's owner, Sam Riddle, who persuaded Arden to get into the horseracing business. One of Man o' War's trainers, Clarence Buxton, even trained Arden's horses for two years.

She also had a connection to the Depression-era Thoroughbred Seabiscuit. Arden hired his trainer, Tom Smith, who ultimately became her longest-tenured trainer—lasting nearly five years before he retired. It was Smith who trained Jet Pilot for the Derby in 1947, a nail-biting race that required the very first photo finish in Kentucky Derby history.

Rein 'Em In

*All about the sport that took Western riding by storm
and may soon be going to the Olympics.*

You've seen reining images on magazine covers for
years: A sleek horse slams to a sliding stop, raising a
cloud of dust. The rider, perfectly balanced, directs his
mount seemingly with just a flick of the wrist. But what
exactly is reining?

The practice was born in the Old West, when horse and
rider needed to be in sync to herd and cut cattle. Since
the 1980s, reining has become increasingly popular as a
sport, leading to rumors that it might soon become an
Olympic event. It's the Western equivalent of dressage,
but faster. Riders in reining competitions guide their
horses through a series of maneuvers (especially circles,
spins, and stops) at a lope and gallop.

Strut Your Stuff

Reining is designed to show off a horse's athleticism and
responsiveness. Competitors are judged on their speed,
accuracy, and finesse at performing specific skills. These
maneuvers are usually part of the competition:

- Walking from the gate to the center of the arena. Poise
  and confidence are what the judges are looking for here.

- Running circles. The circles should be perfectly round at various speeds—large circles at a gallop and small circles at a lope. Judging is based on the circle's form and on how quickly the horse responds to the rider's commands to speed up or slow down.

- Executing a flying lead change (changing the lead at a lope).

- Galloping around the arena, also known as the rundown; this must be performed before a sliding stop.

- Sliding stops—coming to a complete stop by skidding on the hind feet. This has become the iconic image of reining and the most crowd-pleasing trick performed in competition.

- Executing a rollback—making a 180-degree turn immediately after a sliding stop.

- Backing up in a straight line.

- Spinning while keeping one hind leg stationary.

- Pausing between movements and remaining poised and calm.

Got a Quarter?

Any breed of horse can participate in a reining competition, but the most popular is the

American quarter horse. In fact, it was the American Quarter Horse Association that, in 1949, first recognized reining as a sport. Today, the National Reining Horse Association (NRHA) oversees the competitions. In 2000, the NRHA started working with the Federation Equestre Internationale (FEI), the governing board for equestrian events in the Olympics, to get reining on the schedule for the 2012 London Games.

Heavy Medals

The FEI's recognition also helped to increase reining's popularity around the world. It's best known as an American sport, but several countries (including Italy, Israel, Brazil, Canada, and France) hold their own national reining competitions.

The three most prestigious reining competitions are the FEI World Reining Masters, an annual event that began in 2004; the FEI European Championships, held every two years; and the World Equestrian Games (WEG), a major international equestrian competition and the contest that now crowns a World Reining Champion every four years. It was only in 2002 that the WEG even started to include reining, but supporters call it a major step on the road to inclusion in the Olympics. (Of course, some equestrians maintain that the WEG is better than the Olympics anyway.)

Believe It or Not

*You may be surprised at some of the myths
and facts about our four-hoofed friends.*

Seabiscuit was the biggest newsmaker in America in 1938.

Most likely, myth. Laura Hillenbrand made this claim in
her book *Seabiscuit: An American Legend*, which was later
made into a movie. She wrote that in 1938, as the Great
Depression raged and World War II was brewing, more
inches of newspaper column space were devoted to
Seabiscuit than to President Franklin Roosevelt, Adolf
Hitler, or Benito Mussolini. "It's astonishing," Hillenbrand
said in a PBS interview. "I don't think any athlete in history
has ever come close to achieving that. And this is a horse."

However, some people—like Ralph E. Shaffer, profes-
sor emeritus in history at California State Polytechnic
University in Pomona—have challenged her assertion.
Shaffer could not trace Hillenbrand's claim to its original
source. Furthermore, neither a listing in the *San
Francisco News* of more than 100 top headlines of 1938
nor Gallup's public opinion poll of the year's top 10 stories made any reference to Seabiscuit. *The New York
Times Index* and *The Britannica Yearbook* for 1938 contain
few mentions of the racehorse, and these certainly don't

compare in number to the entries about President Roosevelt. But even if Seabiscuit wasn't the top-reported news that year, his story inspired people at a time when they needed it. And he certainly could have been the most discussed topic of casual conversation.

Jell-O is made of horse hooves and bones.

Myth. This is based on something that's true, though: gelatin is derived from the bones and hides of cattle and pigs. Because the ingredients are boiled, filtered, and processed heavily, the final product is not classified as a meat or animal product. But horses are not used in the process.

You can tell a horse's age by its teeth.

Fact. In this case, looking a horse in the mouth has advantages. How many teeth a horse has, the markings and signs of wear on them, and their shape and length all point to a horse's age. A horse is still a foal (under a year old) if it has baby teeth, which are smaller and whiter with a rounded gum line. These start falling out when a foal hits six months. If a horse has a full set of permanent teeth, it's at least four years old. In some horses, a groove appears in their upper corner tooth. Depending on how far down the groove runs, this signifies that a horse is 10, 15, or 20 years old.

For more "believe it or not," turn to page 134.

Training Day

Want to teach an old horse new tricks? Here's some advice.

"Practice sharpens, but overschooling blunts the edge. If your horse isn't doing right, the first place to look is yourself."

—*Joe Heim, horse trainer and breeder*

"The one best precept—the golden rule in dealing with a horse—is never to approach him angrily. Anger is so devoid of forethought that it will often drive a man to do things which in a calmer mood he will regret."

—*Xenophon, ancient Greek writer*

"When your horse has reached his potential, leave it. It is such a nice feeling when you and your horse are still friends."

—*Reiner Klimke, Olympic dressage gold medalist*

"If training has not made a horse more beautiful, nobler in carriage, more attentive in his behavior, revealing pleasure in his own accomplishment . . . then he has not truly been schooled in dressage."

—*Colonel Handler, head of Vienna's Spanish Riding School*

The Little Iron Horses

Thanks to a tenacious poultry farmer–turned politician,
Canada now has an official national horse—
a breed aptly named the Canadian.

A Rugged Horse in a Rugged Land

The saga of the Canadian horse began in 1665 when two
stallions and 20 mares arrived in New France (now Quebec
and the Maritime provinces), a gift from the royal stables of
Louis XIV. The horses quickly adjusted to Canada's extreme
climate, proving themselves to be enduring workhorses and
capable carriage and riding horses. They drew plows on the
prairies and hauled logs from the nation's forests. By the
mid-19th century, the original 22 had multiplied to
150,000. Renowned for their strength and endurance, they
became known as the "Little Iron Horses."

About this time, though, life got tough for the
Canadian breed. They were pressed into service in the
American Civil War, the War of 1812, and the Indian
Wars. Canada's soldiers used them as riding and pack-
horses during the Boer War. In peacetime, they worked as
pack animals during the Klondike gold rush and, on one
occasion, were used on an Arctic expedition. By the end
of the 19th century, their numbers had dwindled, and by
1970, only 400 were registered in Canada.

Comeback Kids

So began an effort to save them. In 1976, breeders in Quebec and Ontario teamed with the University of Guelph's Equine Research Centre to reestablish the stock. Thanks to this work, combined with the horses' resilience, registered Canadians now number about 3,000.

Thank Calder

Getting the breed officially designated "Canada's national horse" took some time. A bill to that effect had been introduced in the Canadian House of Commons in 1994, but it lacked support from someone who really believed in it. Enter Murray Calder, a former horse rancher and poultry farmer who was elected to Canada's Parliament in 1993.

In 1999, Calder reintroduced the bill to make the Canadian the country's national horse, but his colleagues didn't seem to give the idea even a yawn. The bill failed. During the next parliamentary session, Calder tried again—and failed again.

Third Time Lucky

Then, in 2001, Calder found an ally—powerful Canadian senator Lowell Murray, who pushed Calder's bill through the Senate just as Calder reintroduced it in the House. Suddenly, the Canadian horse was a national issue. Heated debate followed:

• Quebec's parliamentary members argued about how the

breed's name was spelled. They felt the French spelling "Canadien" should be used because the horse had originally come from France. That compromise was easy: both spellings would be accepted.

- Then the Albertans jumped in to say the horse didn't represent all of Canada because western Canada's horses had come from south of the border. However, they quieted down when they learned that the Canadian was actually the same breed that had pulled the westbound wagons of Canada's early settlers.

Defying the Status Quo

A third objection had nothing to do with the horse. It centered on the fact that the Senate (who were appointed by the governor general instead of being elected by the people) had approved legislation before the House of Commons (who were elected) had sent it to them. The role of Canada's senate is, for the most part, to rubberstamp legislation already passed by the House. To many people, it looked like Lowell Murray was trying to get around the law. That debate lasted for a while but eventually petered out. Calder's bill finally passed in November 2001, and Canada got its national horse.

* * *

"God forbid that I should go to any heaven where there are no horses." —*R.B. Cunningham-Graham, writer*

Murphy's Law: Horses

- The less time you have, the longer it takes to load the horse into the trailer.
- The more carefully you check the trailer, the more likely the truck will break down.
- As soon as you bring a new hoof pick home, it will disappear.
- If you think you've remembered everything for the horse show, you've forgotten your horse.
- The more people watching, the more your horse will misbehave.
- Your favorite bridle will always break, and the ugliest one will last forever.
- The lighter the horse's coat, the more likely it is to roll in manure the day before a show.
- You will end up with the same number of horses as there are stalls in your barn.
- Your clippers will break when you have one ear left to trim.
- As soon as you've decided on a training program, the riding arena will flood.
- When you're winning, it's time to quit — because the only way to go is down.

Ask Away

Uncle John answers your questions about all things horse.

Why are horses measured to the withers?

A horse's height is measured from the ground to the withers (shoulders)—not the top of its head—because a horse will probably move its head up or down while it is being measured, making an accurate measurement to the head difficult.

Why are horses measured in hands?

Throughout history, human body parts have always provided units of measurement. (In the same way that the foot was used as a measure, the hand has also been used. Ancient Egyptian records, in particular, tend to specify heights in hands.) Over time, horse owners just adopted the hand-measurement technique, and today horses are still mostly measured in hands, although much of Europe (except for England) uses the metric system.

Do horses eat anything strange?

Like humans, horses have dietary preferences. But one menu option that is a bit odd is that some horses sometimes eat . . . er . . . poop. Foals regularly eat their mothers' manure—it is a way for them to learn about their environment and about what is safe for them to eat. Plus, all animals have intestinal parasites that help them break down the food in their digestive tracts. Some of those parasites find their way into the animal's droppings—which, when ingested, populate the eater's own gut.

Why are horses mounted from the left?

This is really just a matter of tradition. In the old days of horsemanship, many men wore swords when they went out on horseback. And because most men were right-handed, they wore their swords on their left side so they could draw them easily with their dominant right hand. With a sword hanging on the left side, it was far safer to mount their horses on the animal's left so the sword didn't get in the way.

Because horses are prey animals instead of predators, their eyes are situated on the sides of their heads rather than in front (like ours). This is because prey animals need to see what's coming at them from all directions. But with eyes on both sides of their heads, horses' visual fields function mostly independently, meaning that a horse does not understand images it receives from its left side the same way it does images from the right. For this reason, horses prefer that repeated activities occur on the same side of their body. But there's no reason a horse couldn't learn to be mounted from the right.

What are the differences among donkeys, mules, and hinnies?

All are members of the *Equidae* (horse) family, but they represent several species. They can interbreed, but their offspring are usually sterile.

- Donkeys were probably domesticated around 3000 BC in Egypt.

- A mule is the offspring of a male donkey and a mare. Mules can be used just like horses, though they have more stamina and leg strength. Mules' reputation for stubbornness is, for the most part, undeserved. They're actually very smart and are usually stubborn only when asked to do something they consider dangerous.

- A hinny is the opposite of a mule: the offspring of a stallion and a female donkey.

* * *

Newborn colts don't eat grass because their long legs make it impossible for their mouths to reach the ground.

Royal Races

*"Ev'ry duke and earl and peer is here; Ev'ryone who
should be here is here." —"Ascot Gavotte," My Fair Lady*

Race: Royal Ascot Races
History: Dates back to 1711
Location: Ascot, England
Racetrack: Ascot Racecourse
Date: June—a five-day event with six races per day. The
first day is always a Tuesday.
Highlight: Day 3 (Ladies' Day) and the Royal Ascot Gold
Cup, the week's longest race.
A Royal Affair: The queen and her entourage usually
attend Ascot, and there is a royal procession every day at
2:00 pm. (People at the race even place bets on what color
the queen's outfit will be each day.)

Traditions

- In the Royal Enclosure, gentlemen must wear full
  morning dress and top hats. Women may not show
  midriffs or bare shoulders, and hats are compulsory.

- Ascot even has a dress code for general-admission
  attendees: women are required "to dress in a manner
  appropriate to a smart occasion." Gentlemen must wear
  a shirt and tie, preferably with a suit or jacket. Strictly

forbidden: sportswear, jeans, and shorts. Another seating area with a less formal atmosphere states, "Whilst we encourage race goers to wear smart clothing, no formal dress code applies."

- Eating is one of the best-loved traditions at Ascot. During the 2003 event, attendees consumed 6,000 lobsters, 120,000 bottles of champagne, and 4.5 tons of strawberries with 550 gallons of cream.

Did You Know?

- Queen Elizabeth is a horse owner, breeder, and avid Ascot fan. Her horses participate in the race, and her jockeys wear purple silks with scarlet sleeves. Best-selling author Dick Francis was once one of the queen's jockeys.
- To get into Ascot's Royal Enclosure (where the queen and her guests sit), visitors need to be sponsored by someone who has a Royal Enclosure badge.

* * *

Tip Your Hat to Him

New Jersey native John Batterson Stetson invented the hat named for him in the 1860s. By 1900, he had the largest hat-making factory in the world. Stetsons became especially popular with cowboys because they were comfortable and handy: some men even used them to scoop water.

The Will to Win

*The bay trotter was called Lovim, but no harness driver
wanted to drive him, let alone love him . . . that is,
until he met a young man named Junior.*

As a harness racer, Lovim should have been a contender
every time he went out of the gate—his exercise times
were consistently fast. But Lovim was a "toe sticker": if he
got into traffic during a race, especially if a sulky cart cut
closely in front of him, he'd stop dead in his tracks. And that
made him a hazard to his driver and to any horse and driver
coming up behind him.

Horse Meets Driver

In 1982, Lovim was nine years old, nearly past his prime.
He was winning just enough to tease his owner, Canadian
Les Rickman, who remained convinced the horse could do
better. But that year, Rickman had a bigger problem: he
couldn't find a driver to take Lovim's reins.

Then he met Don "Junior" MacDonald at Ontario's
Western Fair racetrack. Junior was young (just 22), but he
was already building a solid reputation as a harness driver
and trainer. Junior knew he still had lots to learn, though,
and was eager to work with different horses. So he signed
on to drive Lovim.

It's Not All About Winning

Junior said later that during the first race he was more concerned with keeping Lovim (and himself) out of harm's way than with winning. "We finished far off the pace," he said, "and that was a chore. Lovim knew what he was supposed to be doing—get ahead and stay ahead. Holding him back to keep him out of traffic wore me out."

Even so, Rickman was pleased with Lovim's outing. He hired Junior as the horse's trainer and regular driver. Junior could see that this was a horse who loved to race—he just didn't like other horses in front of him. The two worked hard together, but the toe-sticking continued.

Who's the Boss?

Junior couldn't figure out how to solve the problem until Lovim finally gave him the answer. The pair started a race on the far outside, stayed there throughout—and won. After that, no matter the horse's starting position, Junior put him on the outside as quickly as possible. It worked. Lovim posted eight straight victories.

The horse had another lesson in store for Junior, though. During a race later that season, Lovim was just outside the leader when the sulkies turned down the stretch. The reins slipped from Junior's hands, and he lost control.

But Lovim knew what was expected of him. He didn't deviate. He breezed past the leader and won the race.

Suffering and Unlikely Salvation

By 1984, Les Rickman had sold Lovim, and Junior had moved on to drive and train other horses. Junior had married, and his wife was expecting a baby that December. He also owned a couple of horses of his own—not great champions, but he hoped they'd eventually win enough to pay for their feed and stable fees.

Then, in September 1984, Junior was struck with a fast-moving, debilitating heart disease. Without a heart transplant, doctors told him, he probably wouldn't live to see his baby born. He was just 24, and his name was put on a waiting list for a heart. Within a month of the diagnosis, his spirits had withered almost as much as his body.

In those dark moments, Junior began thinking about Lovim, the horse who, when given a chance, always had the will to win. Lovim had struggled with injuries, yet if called on, he always overcame them. The horse became a powerful spiritual anchor for Junior.

A New Start

On December 13, 1984, Junior got a new heart. Ten days later, his son was born. In January 1985, he was already back at the track—though only as a spectator. His old friend Lovim was on the race card that night.

Unfortunately, Lovim's racing career was nearly over. He'd been dropped down in class to trot in a lowly $1,500 claimer. His decline had been swift. Just a year before, he'd been racing for $7,500 purses. But even at $1,500, he finished out of the money. Lovim was old and arthritic, worn beyond his years. If he was lucky, he might be bought as a buggy horse. If he wasn't lucky, he'd go to a slaughterhouse. Junior wouldn't allow that.

Payback

Before he left the track that night, Junior borrowed enough money to buy Lovim. He had no intention of racing the horse, though. Instead, Junior donated him to the Special Ability Riding Institute, a southern Ontario riding facility for children with disabilities. Lovim took to his new role immediately and soon became a favorite with students.

As for Junior, he retired from racing and training in 1987. Since then, he has traded his reins for golf clubs and his sulky for a golf cart. He is now part-owner of a golf course near Ottawa.

*　　*　　*

Did You Know?

- A horse's teeth take up more space than its brain.
- Horses don't have a gall bladder.
- A horse can't breathe through its mouth.

And the Trophy
Goes To . . .

On page 28, we told you all about the Kentucky Derby.
Here are some odd facts, fun tidbits, and accumulated
knowledge about three other big horse-racing prizes.

The Triple Crown

- No Triple Crown winner is currently still alive.

- The Triple Crown is so difficult to win because all con-
  tenders for the prize must win the Kentucky Derby, the
  Preakness, and the Belmont Stakes. All three races are
  run within a five-week period, making it one of the
  most strenuous events in sports.

- The first trophy to commemorate the Triple Crown was
  crafted in 1950. It was a three-sided vase (each side represented one of the races). This original trophy is on
  display at the Kentucky Derby Museum in Louisville,
  Kentucky. Triple Crown winners today get their own
  personalized trophy, which is engraved with the dates of
  the races won. And the trophy is theirs to keep.

- Since 1875, the first year it was possible to win the
  Triple Crown, only 11 horses have earned the distinc-
  tion. The first, Sir Barton, won in 1919. Other winners
  include Gallant Fox (1930), Omaha (1935), War

Admiral (1937), Whirlaway (1941), Count Fleet (1943), Assault (1946), Citation (1948), Secretariat (1973), Seattle Slew (1977), and Affirmed (1978).

The Preakness

- Biggest upset: Master Derby beat Foolish Pleasure in 1975 . . . at 23–1 odds.

- Since 1940, the winner of the Preakness has received an 18-inch wide, 90-inch long blanket made of black-eyed Susans.

- Only four fillies have won the Preakness: Flocarline (1903), Whimsical (1906), Rhine Maiden (1915), and Nellie Morse (1924).

- At one time, the Preakness had the most valuable trophy in American sports. The Woodlawn Vase—weighing nearly 30 pounds and crafted in 1860 by Tiffany—has been appraised at more than $1 million and originally belonged to Kentucky's now-defunct Woodlawn Racing Association. In 1861, racing aficionados buried it to keep it from being stolen or damaged during the Civil War. After the war, they dug it up, and the trophy changed hands several times until 1917, when it ended up with Thoroughbred owner Thomas C. Clyde, who decided the Maryland Jockey Club, originators of the Preakness, should hand it out as a trophy: race winners could keep the vase for one year and then return it to the club, which would award it to the next winner. But in 1953, the Vanderbilts refused the trophy after winning the Preakness because they didn't want the responsibility of guarding it for the year. After that, racing officials commissioned a Lenox sterling silver replica that winners get to keep. (The original is now on display at the Baltimore Museum of Art.)

- Another Preakness award is the David F. Woods Memorial Award. This one isn't given to a horse, though. It's for the writer of the best Preakness story published in a newspaper, magazine, or journal.

The Belmont Stakes

- Since all Thoroughbred racers can be traced back to three horses—the Darley Arabian, Godolphin Arabian, and Byerley Turk—it makes sense that this racing trophy includes three horses holding up a silver Tiffany bowl. On top of the bowl is a depiction of Fenian, the 1869 Belmont winner and the horse of August Belmont, for whom the race is named. The family kept the bowl until 1926, when they donated it to the race.

- The Belmont has a flower tradition, too. The white carnation is the Belmont's official flower, and 350 of them go into the blanket awarded to the winning horse. (The blanket weighs between 30 and 40 pounds.)

- The most money awarded to a Belmont winner: $1,764,800 to A.P. Indy in 1992.

The Hidden Language of Statues

Rumor has it that there's a secret code embedded in equestrian statues: you can tell how a soldier died by checking the position of the hooves on his horse. Uncle John decided to investigate.

The Myth

Statues of soldiers in heroic poses, often depicted astride formidable steeds, stand in cities all over the United States. The position of the horse's hooves, the story goes, describes how its rider died:

- If both front hooves are in the air, or if the horse is rearing, the soldier died in battle.
- If one hoof is airborne, the rider was wounded in battle—and may (or may not) have died of his wounds at a later time.
- If all four hooves are planted on the ground, the soldier survived the battle and died later of an unrelated cause.

The problem is . . . none of that is true.

The Evidence

Sure, there are many instances where the theories *seem* to hold true. After all, a horse's feet have to be somewhere, and a sculptor has only so many possibilities at his disposal. But in cases that do meet the criteria, says Internet myth debunker snopes.com, the horse's stance and the rider's death match purely by coincidence. In fact, the folks at Snopes surveyed all the equestrian statues in Washington, D.C., and found that just 33 percent follow the convention.

Even more telling are the statues that don't meet the criteria—in particular, two statues of George Washington. In both cases, his horse has one hoof raised. But the Founding Father died in 1799 at his Mount Vernon home. His cause of death: a throat infection unrelated to his military service. Thus, his horse should have had four feet on the ground.

Likewise, Andrew Jackson's statue in Lafayette Park has both legs raised (symbolizing he died in battle), yet he too died at home after retiring from military service. There are statues of Andrew Jackson in Louisiana and Florida that have hooves raised as well.

A statue of Confederate general Stonewall Jackson shows his horse standing erect even though Jackson died in May 1863 after being wounded by his own men. And John J. Pershing's statue in Washington, D.C., has one foot in the air. Pershing, however, was not wounded in battle.

Uncovering the Myth

No one knows for sure how the horse-hooves legend got started, but there is a long tradition of reading meaning into statues' poses. In fact, in England, there is a theory (also false) that the position of arms and legs (crossed or uncrossed) in the statues of English knights identifies them as crusaders (or not) and identifies the number of crusades they participated in.

It seems, though, that the position of horses' legs in statues of American soldiers has more to do with the artist's skill and creative vision than with the way the honoree died. Sculptors have other, more practical factors to consider when designing and executing their monuments. Creating an equestrian statue, for example, is hard work—rearing horse statues are especially difficult because all the weight has to be balanced on the horse's hind legs. In fact, it wasn't until 1852 that equestrian statues even appeared in the United States. The first? Sculptor Clark Mills's Washington, D.C., statue of Andrew Jackson . . . astride a rearing horse.

*   *   *

Social Climbers

Before there were automobiles, horses pulled fire engines, and the animals were usually stabled on a fire station's ground floor. The animals could climb straight stairways, though, and because firemen didn't want them making visits to the upper floors, firehouses started installing circular stairways.

Dude, Where's My Horse?

For more than a century, city slickers have been able to enjoy unspoiled nature, learn new skills, and experience thrills and spills on the back of a horse. All they had to do was sign up for a vacation at a dude ranch.

Teddy Roosevelt Was Some Dude

In 1865, the Civil War finally over, the united country turned its attention to the empty lands out west, and by the 1880s, wealthy urbanites from eastern cities were taking hunting, fly-fishing, and sight-seeing trips there. Theodore Roosevelt headed to North Dakota, where he bought and worked the Maltese Cross Ranch. Even after he became president in 1901, Roosevelt's enthusiasm for the West never left him, and his stories of rugged ranch life inspired a whole generation of eastern "dudes" to spend their vacations ranching.

Around the turn of the 20th century, the romance of horses and cowboys took hold. By the 1920s, the railroads were bringing droves of tourists as far south as Texas and as far west as California. As writers inspired travelers with romantic tales of the region, practical ranchers found a way to keep going when extreme weather, wildfires, and falling cattle prices harmed their profits: they built cabins and hosted trail rides and amateur cattle drives on their properties.

The popularity of these ranches (dubbed "dude" ranches because the term was once slang for a well-dressed man who vacations in the country) continued to grow. And today, they're common vacation sites where suburban families and real urbanites can put on their chaps, take roping lessons, and explore the cowboy lifestyle.

Dudes Down Under

Over the years, dude ranching also spread to far points of the globe—especially Australia and Argentina, where the ranching and cowboy lifestyles still thrive. Visitors to Australia vacation on huge cattle stations that can cover as many as 1 million acres of rough terrain where thousands of cattle graze on the stubby grass.

Escott Station, at the edge of the Gulf of Carpentaria in Queensland, is a place where animals roam amid mango trees for over 1,000 square miles. There, tenderfeet must be prepared for rough-and-ready riding if they want to help muster the cattle for branding or shipping to the market. Escott Station also boasts horses who aren't yet broken, and because Aussie ranches don't have the same insurance liability issues that American ranches do, vacationing dudes can work with the untamed animals.

Ranching with the Gauchos

In the 1600s and 1700s, immigrants from France, Italy, Spain, and Portugal came to Argentina, bringing horses and cattle with them. Some animals escaped from their owners and survived on the country's vast *pampas*—lush lowlands filled with few trees. The population of free horses and cattle on the pampas grew so large that, by the 1700s, *gauchos* (an Indian term meaning "orphans" or "vagabonds") roamed the region, capturing cattle for food and horses for transportation. As the pampas were settled, gauchos started living a nomadic life similar to the cowboys of the American West, working from season to season on the large ranches that spread across Argentina's cattle country.

Today, gauchos still work these ranches (called *estancias*), and many of them take paying guests. On an estancia like Santa Candida on the Uruguay River near Buenos Aires, descendants of Argentina's oldest families—some in the fifth and sixth generation—still hold 1 million acres of land and run thousands of head of cattle. In the more remote Patagonia estancias, at the foot of the Andes, transportation by horse is still a way of life, and vacationers help the gauchos herd cattle.

*   *   *

Scary!

The persistent fear of horses is called "equinophobia."

Lost Breeds, Part 2

Here are two more horse breeds lost to history.

The Norfolk Trotter

The Norfolk trotter first appeared in England around 1750. The animals were known as "travel" horses because they could carry heavy riders for long distances at a fairly fast pace (about 17 mph). They could travel over just about any terrain and were also used as warhorses. Variously known as the Norfolk roadster and the Yorkshire trotter, this breed was the progeny of a racehorse descended from the Darley Arabian.

In 1822, the Norfolk trotter came to America and, through selective breeding with Thoroughbred foundation sires, produced a number of other famous breeds: the stan-dardbred, the Hackney, the Shales, and the Missouri fox trotter. No one knows exactly when the Norfolk trotter became extinct, but crossbreeding continued to dilute the bloodline until the original breed was lost.

The Yorkshire Coach

The Yorkshire coach was born from crossing Cleveland bays and Thoroughbreds to produce stronger, faster, more elegant carriage horses. Cleveland bays weren't fast or stylish enough for this prestigious position, but they had an exceptional disposition. Thoroughbreds were considered prettier, faster, and classier, but much too temperamental to be carriage horses. So breeders crossed the two to get the best characteristics of both. The Yorkshire coach was the result and became the preferred breed for carriage horses—especially in 18th-century London.

Colorful coaches, drivers, and horses decorated the city's Hyde Park in those days, and the Yorkshire coach made quite an impression. The breed was handsome—typically brown or bay with a thick mane and tail, black eyes, and lengthy quarters. They stood 16 to 16.2 hands tall and high-stepped with grace and pride, almost excessively prim and proper, even by the standards of the day.

This is another breed that was lost through crossbreeding, but its foundation breeds still exist. So Yorkshire coach horses could be reintroduced, if someone were inclined to make the effort.

For more extinct horses, turn to page 23.

Bad Boys (and Girls) of the Rodeo

Meet three of the sport's greats.

The Bulldogger

In 1971, Bill Pickett was the first African American inducted into the National Rodeo Hall of Fame in Oklahoma. More than 75 years after his death, he is still recognized as one of rodeo's greatest innovators.

Learning the ropes: Pickett was born in Texas in 1870. He became a ranch worker early on (around the age of 10) and started riding horses about the same time. His big break came in 1905 when he got a job performing in the wildly popular 101 Ranch Wild West Show, which included Buffalo Bill Cody and Will Rogers. Pickett soon became one of the show's most popular stars.

Signature move: Pickett pioneered bulldogging (steer wrestling) as a rodeo event. The dangerous activity involved Pickett galloping his horse, Spradley, alongside a longhorn steer and wrestling with the animal until it was under control. One of Pickett's methods for getting the steer to submit: he bit its upper lip.

Roundup: Pickett died in 1932 after being kicked in the

head by a horse. In 1989, he was inducted into the Pro Rodeo Hall of Fame and the Museum of the American Cowboy in Colorado. Five years later, the United States Postal Service gave him his own stamp. (But the USPS goofed and used his brother's picture instead of his.) Pickett's name is also attached to the only touring rodeo of African Americans in the United States today—the Bill Pickett Invitational Rodeo.

The Champion Lady Bucking Horse Rider

A proud woman who refused to settle for anything (in or out of the rodeo circuit), Lulu Bell Parr kicked up a lot of dust. She was outspoken, a supporter of women's rights, and one of the most accomplished bucking bronco riders of her time.

Learning the ropes: Parr was born in 1876 in Indiana, and after her parents split up, she moved west with her father. There, she learned to love horses, and at the age of 27— after divorcing her first husband for what she called "extreme cruelty"—she joined the Pawnee Bill Wild West Show. She stayed for four years (until 1907) and then traveled to Europe as part of Colonel F. T. Cummins's Wild West Brighten Tour. When she returned to the States in 1910, she joined the Two Bill Show (or, as the combined rodeo extravaganza was formally known, Buffalo Bill's Wild West–Pawnee Bill's Far East Show). The show dubbed Parr the "Champion Lady Bucking Horse Rider of the World," and she dazzled audiences with her act: riding bucking broncos and buffalo, performing tricks, and sharpshooting.

A noteworthy mention: Parr wasn't just a rodeo queen. In May 1913, the *Hanover* (Pennsylvania) *Herald* profiled her and called her large ranch in Nebraska "one of the most productive in the state." The paper also noted Parr's commitment to women's voting rights: "She . . . is a suffragette in every sense of the word."

Roundup: Parr continued to ride with various rodeos until she retired in her 60s. But by then, she was broke (the result of less money being paid out on the dwindling rodeo circuit) and had to move in with her brother and sister-in-law. The three lived in a tar-paper home with no electricity, but Parr still managed to entertain the neighborhood: dressed in her flashy costumes, she dazzled locals with tales of her performing days.

Lulu Parr died in 1955. She's buried in Medway, Ohio, and in 2005, she was inducted into the National Cowgirl Hall of Fame.

The Ultimate Cowboy

Larry Mahan was only 14 in 1957, when he competed in his first rodeo. It was just a kids' calf-riding competition, but he won it, setting the stage for many more victories. Seven years later, he went pro and, in 1966, won the first of five consecutive all-around championships—the award given to the top-earning member of the Professional Rodeo Cowboys Association. He won the title again in 1973, setting a record that stood until Ty Murray bested it in 1994.

Show him the money: Mahan was the top bull-riding money winner in 1965. And in 1967, he won more than $50,000, the first rodeo rider to do so in a single year. By the time he retired in 1977, he'd taken home $250,000 from rodeos, a record accomplishment at the time.

Noteworthy mention: Perhaps Mahan's most notable accomplishment, though, is the fact that he lived his rodeo life for 20 years without sustaining a major injury. Even more impressive: in 1,200 rodeos, Mahan regularly competed in the three most dangerous events—bullriding (which causes half of all rodeo injuries), bareback riding, and saddle bronc riding.

Roundup: Mahan became one of the modern rodeo's first stars. In 1973, he was the subject of an Academy Award–winning documentary called *The Great American Cowboy*. And he released an album in 1976: *Larry Mahan, King of the Rodeo*. Today, he sells clothes (the Larry Mahan Line of Western wear) and hosts a television program called *Equestrian Nation*. And he's been inducted into the Pro Rodeo Hall of Fame, the National Cowboy and Western Heritage Museum's Rodeo Hall of Fame, the Oregon Sports Hall of Fame, and the Texas Cowboy Hall of Fame.

For Horse Lovers Only

More "you know you're a horse person when . . ."

- In the grocery store, you move someone aside by poking them and saying "over."
- You walk out in the middle of a movie because the "cowboy" flaps his elbows at the trot.
- You see a jogger on the street, and think some corrective shoeing might help that hitch in his gait.
- You're too sick to work, but think a two-hour ride will do you good.
- You watched *Bonanza* as a kid because you had a crush on Michael Landon's horse.
- You look at a picture of Santa's reindeer and think, "They'll never clear that jump if they don't pick up their knees."
- You buy shirts to match the color of your horse's slobber.
- You have a saddle-soap stain on the living room rug.
- You're thinking of living in the barn since it's cleaner than the house.
- You clean the tack after every ride, but you've never washed the car.

The Rise and Fall (and Rise) of Draft Horses

On page 114, we'll tell you about the famous Clydesdales, but draft horses in general have their own story. Fortune and "progress" took them from indispensable to nearly extinct in less than 100 years. Here's the story of where they came from . . . and how they managed to come back.

Drafted

Draft horses developed in north central Europe around AD 1000. Their ancestors were strong, fast warhorses called *destriers*, who provided the bloodline that produced the "Black Horse of Flanders," the forerunner of the modern draft breeds.

Initially, draft horses were used mostly on European farms. Early American colonists used oxen instead—an ox was usually cheaper (about half the cost of a horse), ate less, and, in lean years, could be eaten if necessary. But oxen were slower workers than horses, and their small hooves often left them helpless on America's marshy northern and eastern terrain. Draft horses, though, had hooves about twice the diameter of riding horses, and they were strong and hardy. So as pioneers moved west, they started taking draft horses with them.

Draft Horse Heyday

By the late 1800s, tens of thousands of draft horses had been imported from western Europe and were being bred throughout the United States. Within about a decade, breeders had even created the American cream draft, the first draft horse developed exclusively in the United States.

Midwestern grain farmers owned an average of 10 draft horses in the early 1900s and used the animals to power plows, combines, and threshing machines. At harvest time, teams of up to 40 draft horses brought in the crop. Draft horses found work on the railroad, too, carrying supplies to the work site and then hauling away the excavated dirt and rock.

As more people moved to the cities, they needed transportation—and again called on draft horses. More than 100,000 of them powered the horsecar lines that operated in every major American city by the turn of the 20th century. They also pulled steam pumps and ladder trucks used by early fire departments. And many well-to-do city dwellers maintained personal stables with four or six stately draft horses who pulled ornate carriages around town.

Down But Not Out

And then came cars, trucks, tractors, and electric streetcars, and draft horses mostly disappeared from view. They continued to thrive in some out-of-the-way places. In the United States, Amish and Mennonite farmers played a big part in keeping many draft horses, especially the Percheron, from extinction. Even today, these farmers own thousands of draft horses who work their fields and pull their carriages.

Draft horses were key players in World War I, when more than 500,000 were called into service. The heavy horses delivered supplies and ammunition and hauled heavy artillery to the front.

By the 1960s, draft horses were making a real comeback. The animals are strong and sure-footed, and people soon found new work for them. In particular, they proved to be more efficient than trucks in extracting downed trees and pulling stumps in logging operations. Nowadays, beautiful examples of many breeds—Belgians, Shires, Percherons, Friesians, and others—can be seen at prestigious draft horse shows around the country.

What a Beauty

One saving grace for these horses is that they are gentle, friendly, and attractive. Some draft breeds make good riding horses, especially in Western and dressage, and are lauded for their smooth gait. And the long manes and tails and feathered legs of some breeds have even earned them the nickname fairy-tale horses.

Inspiring Horse Tails

*Here are two animals who got a second chance
thanks to some very special people.*

Saving Straight Flush

World-famous racehorse Secretariat had a half-brother
named Straight Flush. But despite being related to one of
the most famous horses in history, in 1999 Straight Flush
was on his way to a slaughterhouse in Pennsylvania.
That's when a writer named Stephanie Diaz stepped in
and saved him.

Straight Flush was born in 1975 and started racing as a
two-year-old. In spite of his pedigree (Secretariat as a half-
brother, Somethingroyal as his dam, and Riva Ridge as his
sire), he just wasn't a great racehorse. He lost every race
he entered during his first season, but finally won at Santa
Anita in 1978 (with Bill Shoemaker riding him). But that
was the best he could do. Straight Flush won a couple of
smaller races, but he never lived up to the potential everyone thought he had. Within a few months, his owner had
sold him.

To the Highest Bidder: Over the next two decades,
Straight Flush moved from farm to farm. He went to stud,
but didn't have much success. Finally, in 1999, he ended up

at a feed lot·in Texas and was put up for auction on the Internet. That's how Diaz got involved. A friend let her know that Secretariat's half-brother was for sale and had no interested buyers. So she bid $200 and waited. Within a few days, she found out she'd won the auction—and the horse.

Diaz arranged to pick up Straight Flush in Texas and have him moved to California, where he lived for the next eight years. He was in rough shape—and didn't have many teeth—but he lived out the rest of his days in a good home. Straight Flush died on September 3, 2007, at the incredible age of 32.(Most racehorses don't make it past 20.)

My Little Pony

No one knows for sure where Molly came from, but in 2005, the gray-speckled, 16-year-old Appaloosa pony was found wandering alone in Louisiana after Hurricane Katrina. She ended up at the home of Kaye Harris, who fostered horses and other animals. Molly seemed to be doing all right in Harris's care until, one day, a pit bull terrier that Harris also fostered attacked the pony in the yard. By the time Harris arrived, Molly was severely injured: her stomach was badly cut, all four legs had been bitten, and the dog was gnawing at her jaw. Harris managed to get the dog to let Molly go, but the pony didn't look like she was going to make it.

Harris rushed Molly to a local vet, who patched her up. But when the pony got an infection in her right front leg, Harris took her to the Louisiana State University veterinary hospital. Doctors there initially thought she'd have to be euthanized, and Harris knew that the odds were against a full recovery. "[Treating a pony with an injured leg is] so expensive," she said, "and so hard, and everyone who tries fails. But we just asked them to spend some time with Molly."

The doctors at LSU fell in love with the pony. She had a sweet disposition and got along well with everyone, even in her injured state. They decided to amputate her leg and fit her for a prosthesis, which was donated to the cause.

A Miraculous Recovery: Today, more than two years after her surgery, Molly is fine. She can walk with and without her prosthetic limb, and also works as a therapy pony— Harris takes her to hospitals, nursing homes, any place whose residents need a good story to brighten their day. In particular, children with prosthetic limbs respond to Molly's story so well that she's even become the subject of a book: *Molly the Pony* was released in 2008.

And what about the dog who attacked her? Harris was convinced that his outburst was the result of trauma caused by the hurricane. Rather than have him euthanized, she found him a home with a family trained to deal with troubled dogs.

The King of Games

When most people think of polo, they envision a team of English gentlemen in striped knickers and shirts, riding horses in an open field and swinging their clubs at a tiny white ball. OK...that's not a bad description, but there's much more to the sport than that.

4

Number of players on an outdoor polo team. All players are on the field throughout the game, and they play numbered positions (1–4), which are sewn on their team jerseys. Position one is the lead offensive player (like a forward in soccer). Position two is mostly offensive but also plays defense. Position three attacks the opposing team's offense and is usually his team's captain. And position four defends his team's goal. (Indoor polo teams usually have three players; they combine positions two and three.)

7½ minutes

Length of a regulation polo period (called a chukker).

6 to 8

Number of polo ponies each player uses during a game. Full games last eight chukkers, club games usually last six, and players generally use a different horse for each chukker to keep the animals fresh and alert. (The horses are called "polo ponies," but that's just tradition. They're actually horses, and many are Thoroughbreds.)

10 acres
The size of a regulation outdoor polo field: 300 yards long by 160 yards wide—about the size of nine football fields. Indoor fields are 100 yards by 50 yards.

77
Countries where people play polo. These include England, India, Argentina, Brazil, France, Canada, the United States, several Caribbean countries, and many Arab nations. There are at least 10,000 registered players worldwide, though many polo experts say there are closer to 50 million (mostly unregistered) players around the globe.

600 BC
Year of the first recorded polo match. Opponents: the Turkmen and the Persians. (The Turkmen won). No one knows why they played this match, but more than two centuries later in 336 BC, Darius III, the emperor of Persia, sent a polo mallet and ball to Alexander the Great with a message that said, roughly, "Play polo, not war." And an ancient stone tablet, found near a polo field north of Kashmir, was inscribed with this verse: "Let other people play at other things—the king of games is still the game of kings."

1975

Year that left-handers were officially banned from the game of polo for safety reasons. Southpaws swing their polo sticks in the opposite direction of right-handers, which can cause serious accidents.

1982

Year the World Elephant Polo Association (WEPA) formed in southwest Nepal. The tradition of playing polo from the backs of elephants, instead of horses, began at the turn of the 20th century in India, where there were few horses—but many elephants. Elephant polo is now a professional sport. The WEPA sponsors a world championship in Nepal every winter, and the Thai Elephant Polo Association sponsors global tournaments in Thailand every September.

$5,000

Average price of a good polo pony, generally one that's 10 to 12 years old. But they can range from $1,500 to more than $100,000 (the priciest ones usually just show up in prestigious matches).

$174,000

Average annual income for a professional polo player. The tops riders, though, earn $500,000 or more through sponsorships, endorsements, and their match winnings.

Track Duty

You know about trainers and owners, and we've told you about jockeys (on page 28) and grooms (on page 191). But what about the other people who make a racetrack or stable run smoothly? See if you can choose the correct title based on the job description. (Hint: Some of these jobs are international.)

1. Buys and sells horses. Must be an expert in racing, pedigree, athleticism, bodywork, and the horse market in general. Special skills: marketing and sales.
a. Trainer
b. Bloodstock agent
c. Breed broker

2. Oversees a stable's breeding program and maintains breeding records.
a. Stud foreman
b. Track clerk
c. Stock keeper

3. Operates the vehicles that move horses from one place to another. Must be experienced with horses and time management because he or she needs to make sure the horses get to their destinations on time and that transportation records are accurate.

a. Skinner
b. Community coach
c. Float driver

4. Gives people the opportunity to see different areas on horseback. Must possess exceptional horsemanship skills and get along well with other people.
a. Horse trek guide
b. Outrider
c. Rawhider

5. Typically an early morning job. Exercises and helps to train horses and reports back to the main trainer about the horses' progress.
a. Dawn rider
b. Trackwork rider
c. Steward

6. Can be part of a groom's job but is sometimes a separate position position. This person cools horses down after exercise or a race.
a. Late trainer
b. Stable boy
c. Hot walker

For answers, turn to page 222.

Horsing Around

*While we were studying all the serious subjects
for this book, we found these jokes.*

What's the best kind of story to tell a runaway horse?
A tale of WHOA!

What did the horse say when it fell?
I've fallen, and I can't giddyap!

**What's the vampire's favorite
part of a horse race?**
When it's neck and neck.

**What breeds of horses can
jump higher than a house?**
All breeds. Houses don't jump.

Why can't horses dance?
Because they have two left
feet.

Why can't a pony sing?
Because he's a little hoarse.

Boot Camp

*Now an American staple, riding and cowboy
boots owe a lot to European history.*

Riding High

Boots have always played a role in the footwear of
humankind—cave paintings dating back as many as
15,000 years show men and women wearing them. But
by the 16th century, boots were mostly worn by soldiers,
who needed to protect their feet and legs on the battlefield. Knights often wore boots up to their thighs to protect their knees. Over the years, boots moved into the
general population, and nonmilitary riders usually preferred knee-highs—they were high enough to protect
the lower legs from chafing but not so high that they
interfered with riding.

   During the 17th century, boots became increasingly popular in Europe. Royals and other elites liked to raise and
ride horses, and the boots they wore while riding came to
signify status. In particular, the size of the boot's heel was
important. Riding boots came with heels of up to three
inches—leading to the term "well-heeled" to show that a
person was rich enough to own a horse. The thicker the
heel, the thinking went, the wealthier the person was.

Beef Wellington

By the 1800s, riding boots were common among wealthy cavalry officers, and even among some regular citizens. But they could be uncomfortable, especially thigh-high military boots. Then came Arthur Wellesley, the first Duke of Wellington, who decided to change that.

When Wellington defeated Napoleon at the Battle of Waterloo in 1815, he didn't just strike a blow for England, he also made a case for fashion. He didn't like the military boots he had been issued, so he directed his cobbler to create something calf-length, to offer a tighter fit around the legs. His boots (which came to be called Wellingtons) also had a lower heel than typical riding boots to make it easier for the rider when he wasn't in the saddle—higher heels stay in place better while riding, but aren't as great to walk (or fight battles) in. Plus, the boots were easy to mass-produce. Soon, riders all over Europe and the United States were wearing Wellingtons.

Northern and Southern soldiers wore Wellingtons during the Civil War, and the boots were so well received that, when the men returned home, they brought their footwear with them. It was perfect timing. The cattle and beef industry in America was booming in the late 1860s, and the cowboys who herded the cattle needed a comfortable boot.

Feet First

Before the 1860s, cowboys had to put up with a lot in their footwear. Mostly, they had to sacrifice comfort for function: that high heel again. Many boots also had very pointy toes, which made them fit more easily into stirrups, but pinched the rider's feet when he was out of the saddle.

But after the Civil War, Buffalo Bill Cody, Wild Bill Hickok, and other cowboys started wearing Wellingtons, which led to an evolution in cowboy boots. Over time, the boots developed a lower heel and more rounded toe, and had a slicker sole that helped the cowboy slip out of his stirrups quickly if a horse got out of control. From there, riding and cowboy boot evolution was pretty much complete. Over the last 150 years, boots have changed very little, and the basic medium-heeled, slightly rounded-toe style remains popular.

* * *

The Cowboy's Prayer

May your horse never stumble,
Your spurs never rust,
May your guts never grumble,
Your cinch never bust!

May your boots never pinch,
Your crops never fail,
While you eat lots of beans,
And stay out of jail!

Clop, Clop, Clop

Here come the Clydesdales!

- The breed originated in Scotland around 1750 in an area known as the Clyde valley. Flemish stallions were crossed with native Scottish mares to produce large, heavy draft horses who could do farmwork and haul the region's coal.

- A stallion named Blaze, foaled in 1779, is the breed's foundation sire. He stood 16.1 hands and had the two markings that Clydesdales have become known for: a white blaze on his face and four white feet.

- On average, Clydesdales stand between 16 and 18 hands tall and weigh 1,600 to 1,800 pounds.

- Anheuser-Busch, the maker of Budweiser beer, maintains the largest herd of Clydesdales in the world: approximately 250 horses.

- A team of six Clydesdales first pulled an Anheuser-Busch wagon (filled with beer from the company's St. Louis brewery) in 1933 to celebrate the repeal of Prohibition. Since then, the horses and hitch teams have become the beer company's primary mascots. The horses appear in print ads, marketing materials, and, of course, those Super Bowl commercials.

- In the early 1950s, Anheuser-Busch added a new animal to its Clydesdale teams—Dalmatians were fast enough to keep up with the horses and were trained to guard the wagons when drivers had to leave them unattended. Recently, the dalmatians have appeared with the Clydesdales in a series of television commercials.

To read more about draft horses, turn to page 99.

*　　*　　*

Horsey Q & A

Q: Why do velvet riding helmets have a bow at the back?

A: Like so many things, the bow once had historical significance but now is just tradition. The English started putting ribbons on their hunting hats in the 1700s. The color of the ribbon denoted the type of hunting: fox hunters wore black ribbons; stag hunters wore red. The ribbons' length showed the hunters' societal status: Only hunt masters and their staff were allowed to have the ends of their ribbons hang below the edges of their helmets. Commoners had to cut off or glue down the tails of their ribbons, and it was a great faux pas for the "wrong" person to have the wrong ribbon length.

Born Free

*On page 17, we introduced the wild ponies of Assateague
and Chincoteague. Here are two more feral herds
that run free along America's East Coast.*

Banker Horses

Today, the Outer Banks, a group of islands off the coast of
North Carolina that shelter the state's shore from the
Atlantic, are connected to the mainland by a bridge. But
for hundreds of years, the islands were isolated . . . and so
were the horses who lived there. No one seems to know
for sure when they arrived. Local lore says they were shipwreck survivors, but it's more likely they came over in the
1520s when the Spanish tried to colonize the area.

Today, about 400 horses still live on the Outer Banks,
and the group has been recognized as its own breed. The
Bankers look a lot like Spanish horses: they're small (14 to
15 hands tall and 800 to 1,000 pounds) and have broad
foreheads, strong backs, and silky tails and manes. They're
also generally calm and friendly and take well to domesti-
cation if captured—in fact, during the late 19th and early
20th centuries, mainlanders regularly rounded up the
horses and sold them at auctions.

Banker horses adapted well over the years, and the
seashore has become their natural habitat. But as people

moved onto the islands, the horses had less room to roam, so locals have started moving the animals to uninhabited areas where they can be protected. On a few of the islands, the National Park Service looks after them.

Cumberland Island Horses

Off the southern coast of Georgia lies 18-mile long Cumberland Island. Most of it is undeveloped and under the protection of the National Park Service, but the rest is owned by the Carnegie family, who used it as a retreat in the early 1900s. Before that, the island hosted an English fort and then the home of Revolutionary War general Nathanael Greene, whose widow built a mansion called Dungeness there. The mansion burned to the ground during the Civil War, but its stone walls and chimneys remain and are a frequent grazing spot for the island's feral horses.

On Cumberland, the horses rule. Cars aren't allowed (except National Park vehicles), and rangers warn visitors to yield to horses in their path—the animals are used to human visitors, but they aren't used to changing their habits to suit the tourists. The original stock probably came from 16th-century Spanish explorers, and over the years, the island's various residents introduced new breeds, too. Today, about 250 horses live on the island.

Cumberland Island horses look a lot like Banker horses but are usually a little larger. And they have long, "scooper"- like toes . . . all the better for galloping over the island's deep sand dunes.

Donkey Down Under

This knock-kneed fellow has made quite an impression on his country-mates.

On March 29, 2008, the folks at Australia's Willowdale Donkey Stud farm witnessed a rare event: a jenny named Fantasy had twins, only the fourth such pair known to survive anywhere in the world. According to Willowdale's owner, Barbara Bracken, "Equines don't carry twins. They either abort both at six months or give birth to one live and one stillborn."

These babies (named Donegan and Lonegan) both made it, but Lonegan was severely knock-kneed. It had been so crowded inside his mother's womb that his legs never developed properly. He had trouble walking, and the disability put extra strain on his shoulders and back.

Aussies to the Rescue

Historically, such disabled animals were euthanized because they made poor workers. But Bracken wasn't willing to give up on Lonegan. She took him to veterinary specialists who said they could fix the foal's legs, but it would be costly . . . thousands of dollars. So she set up a Web site and contacted local news stations. Before long, Lonegan's story was front-page news, and people from all over Australia were sending money to support his treatment.

Today, the little donkey walks around in casts used to straighten and strengthen his front legs. He'll need at least three more years of treatment, Bracken says, including surgery to insert pins into his knees to keep them straight. But thanks to the support of his countrymen, more than $30,000 in donations will pay for his care.

*   *   *

A Horse of a Different Stripe

- No two zebras have exactly the same stripes. (Their stripes are as distinct as human fingerprints.)
- The stripes are also a form of camouflage. In the wild, lions are a zebra's main predator, and since lions are color blind, a zebra standing in tall grass or a herd moving together, especially at dawn and dusk, is hard for a lion to see clearly.
- Many zebras can run up to 40 mph.
- Average zebra life span: 28 years.
- Are they black with white stripes, or with with black stripes? The common thinking is that zebras are white with black stripes because the stripes usually end at their bellies and the insides of their legs (which are all white).
- Zebra foals can walk just 20 minutes after they're born.
- A zebra's eyesight at night is about as good as a cat's or an owl's.

Horse Power of a Different Kind

For centuries, cultures around the world have sworn by these sometimes-contradictory horse superstitions.

Protection and Good Luck

- Everyone knows it's bad luck to walk under a ladder, but you can also avoid the bad if you keep your fingers crossed until you have seen three horses.
- If you break a mirror in the house or spill salt in the kitchen, any ensuing misfortune can be averted if you lead a horse through the house.
- Horse brasses (decorative harness plaques) protect a horse from witches and humans from the evil eye.
- For protection from witches, wear a black stallion's tail hair on your wrist.

Curses and Cures

- If a horse neighs at your door, you will get sick.
- To cure warts, circle them in horse hair.
- Eat hair from a horse's forelock to cure worms.
- Inhale a horse's breath to cure whooping cough, or put three hairs from a donkey's shoulder into a muslin bag and wear it around your neck. (This also cures measles.)

Color

- Seeing one white horse is bad luck—unless you are with your lover, in which case, it is good luck.
- Seeing two white horses together will bring you good luck. (Whether you're with a lover or not.)
- Seeing a piebald horse is also good luck—unless you first see his tail up, which means you will have bad luck instead.
- In England and Germany, dreaming of a white horse is considered a death omen.
- We know meeting a white horse can be lucky or unlucky, but there are protocols to follow in either case—spit and make a wish (lucky), or cross your fingers until you see a dog (unlucky).
- Seeing a gray horse on the way to a church is considered good luck for a bride and groom. Gray horses are supposed to be lucky in general—except in Wales, where they are omens of death.

Hodgepodge

- Don't change your horse's name; it's bad luck.
- If a pregnant woman sees a donkey, her child will grow up to be wise and well behaved.
- If you see a white dog, remain silent until you see a white horse.
- The deeper a horse dips his nostrils while drinking, the better sire he will be.

Przewalski's Horses

Introducing . . . the only horse breed
never to be domesticated.

Przewalski horses, called the *taki* ("spirit") in
Mongolian—are native to Central Asia. The horses
got their modern name from Nikolai Przewalski, a Russian
explorer who visited Mongolia in the mid-19th century
and found two herds near the Gobi Desert.

What Makes Them Different?

Przewalskis are small—they weigh between 450 and 750
pounds and typically stand 12 to 14 hands tall. A dark
stripe, called an "eel stripe," runs down their backs.
Przewalskis also have unusually sharp hooves that they use
to defend themselves and to dig up water from the rocky
ground in the grassy deserts and treeless steppes of western
Mongolia. And, interestingly, they they have 66 chromo-
somes, rather than the 64 other horse breeds have.

Przewalskis are hard to capture, but in the early 1900s, a
few people caught about 100 and imported them to
Europe. Only 53 survived the journey, and just 13 of those
thrived in captivity. All of the nearly 1,500 Przewalskis in
captivity today trace their family trees to one of those 13.

To the Rescue!

Life after the races can be deadly for horses, but some rescue groups are trying to change that.

Ferdinand's story was the stuff of legend. Before the 1986 Kentucky Derby, the three-year-old chestnut Thoroughbred was a 17–1 long shot. His win defied expectations and set records: the oldest jockey ever to win the contest (Bill Shoemaker, age 54) and largest purse at that time ever paid out to the winner ($609,500). Ferdinand went on to place second in the Preakness and third in the Belmont Stakes that year. And in 1987, he was named Horse of the Year after the Breeders' Cup Classic.

But Ferdinand's story took a tragic turn after that. When he was retired from racing in 1989, he was sent to stud, but his offspring never proved to be as fast or skilled on the racetrack as he was. So in the mid-1990s, he was shipped off to Japan, where breeders again tried to put him up for stud. No luck. Finally, in 2002, the Kentucky Derby winner was sent to a Japanese slaughterhouse.

The Ugly Side

Ferdinand wasn't the only one. Roughly 100,000 American horses are sold to slaughterhouses overseas every year, and about 15,000 of those are Thoroughbreds. The situation used to be even worse. It wasn't until 2007 that the U.S. Department of Agriculture stopped inspecting horse meat. Because inspection is required for any meat processing done in the United States, that decision put an end to the country's three horse-meat processing plants (one in Illinois and two in Texas). But even though slaughter-houses in the United States have shut down, it's still an easy trip over the border into Mexico or Canada, where thousands of horses are killed for meat every year.

Each horse sold to a slaughterhouse brings up to $500, but it costs about $5,000 a year to feed, shelter, and care for a horse. And even though some horses, like Ferdinand, earn big payouts in their day, many owners decide that the horses will cost more than they're worth. So, given the choice of paying to put a horse down, paying for it to live out its natural life, or earning a little cash by getting rid of the animal, many owners choose the latter. And because of that trend, rescue organizations all over the United States are stepping in and trying to change owners' minds about how to handle horses that don't fit the standard definition of high performers.

On the Mend

Dozens of these groups exist around the country. Some are dedicated especially to Thoroughbreds; others will take in any breed. But they all share similar goals: to end the slaughter of American horses and to give all the animals good homes where they can live out their days.

The horse lovers who run the rescue groups pride themselves on giving the horses as simple and carefree a life as possible. They reintroduce the animals to living among herds, where they don't have to race or do heavy work. Many horses arrive with injuries sustained during their racing days, and some even have to go through detox to flush out steroids and other performance-enhancing drugs in their systems.

Adoption Service

One of the largest Thoroughbred rescuers is CANTER, a free Michigan-based service established in 1997 that helps to match needy horses with nonracing people who want them. Jo Anne Normile had her own racehorses, whom she turned into eventing horses when the animals' track careers were finished. At the track, Normile and her husband met many trainers and owners who wanted to sell their former racehorses rather than send them to slaughterhouses. So the Normiles started CANTER. There are now offices in six other states, and the group gives support and advice to both sellers and owners.

CANTER and other groups usually operate at full capacity all year, but they're still only able to help a small percentage of the total number of needy horses and rely mostly on outside donations to continue their operations. But as the plight of unwanted horses becomes better known, additional resources become available, making the obstacles a little less intimidating.

The Almighty Stirrup?

According to one historian, the stirrup had far-reaching historical consequences. (We're not so sure.)

With the exception of standing in the saddle at a full gallop, it's possible to do almost everything on horseback without stirrups that a rider can do with them (even post)—it's just more difficult. Some of the greatest cavalries in history rode without stirrups, and Alexander the Great conquered most of the world without them. But given that the rung serves as a step for mounting, a footrest during long rides, and an added means of control and stability, it's no wonder that once stirrups caught on, few horsemen wanted to ride without them.

A Step Up

Officially, stirrups were invented in China in the 4th century AD, though some archaeologists offer evidence that the Assyrians used them much earlier, around 850 BC. Stirrups came to eastern Europe in the 7th century AD by way of invading tribes and immediately caught on with people there because they made most aspects of horseback riding so much easier.

One 20th-century historian, though, argued that stirrups were much more than just a convenience. In 1962, Lynn White Jr. went so far as to claim they were among the most historically important inventions of all time. White wrote, "Few inventions have been so simple as the stirrup, but few have had so catalytic an influence on history."

A Feudal Invention?

White's argument was complicated, but the short version goes like this: stirrups led to the advent of feudalism, the medieval political system that set up strict economic class divisions in Europe. Horses had been used in war for a long time, but according to White, the adoption of the stirrup in the 8th century made it possible for soldiers to use "shock tactics"—charging an enemy on horseback with the full weight of the animal behind the attack. This was an effective war maneuver, and it caused a shift in how armies fought: they went from relying on infantry (men on the ground) to putting more stock in their cavalries, which had the advantage. (They were faster, stronger, and more in control of the fight.)

But all these new, elite cavalry officers needed an incentive to drop everything and rush to the battlefield whenever their leaders called on them—which was pretty often because Europe was filled with warring tribes and invaders at the time. So to ensure the cavalry officers' loyalty, the monarchs (first in France and then throughout Europe) granted them large parcels of land to lord over. And because the landowners couldn't work all that land themselves, they needed cheap laborers (who became known as serfs) to do it. Voilà! Feudalism.

That Sounds Good, But . . .

When White published his hypothesis in 1962, it caused quite a ruckus among medieval historians who all clamored to prove or disprove his theory. Ultimately, most of them rejected his argument for two reasons:

- It's possible to use shock tactics without stirrups. More important for this style of fighting is the saddle's cantle: the rider can brace against it at the point of impact. The cantle was around much earlier than the stirrup—even the Romans used it. Plus, modern riders have been able to joust bareback without being unhorsed, proving that the stirrup is not essential for a successful cavalry.

- Second, the first record of Europeans using shock tactics is at the 1066 Battle of Hastings. Stirrups were around long before that, so there's no clear evidence that the arrival of the stirrup and the use of shock tactics coincided. In fact, the only clear military advantage the stirrup provided was for mounted archers—by standing up in the stirrups, an archer could improve his aim.

In the end, White's hypothesis seemed off-base, and most historians today believe that, even though the stirrup did provide a huge convenience for riders and cavalries, and even aided soldiers during wartime, it wasn't the root of feudalism.

Horses of the Dunes

These horses roam wild, reject feed touched by human hands, and survive in the "Graveyard of the Atlantic"—a desolate crescent of sand dunes known as Sable Island.

Sable Island is a 20-mile-long sandbar lurking in the North Atlantic Ocean, about 100 miles off the coast of Nova Scotia. Since the 17th century, hundreds of ships and thousands of crew and passengers have met their end on Sable's treacherous, ever-shifting shoals. Yet among that destruction lives a population of horses who have survived the elements for more than two centuries.

Some of the Sable Island horses were probably survivors of early shipwrecks. Others were transported there during fruitless attempts to colonize the island—first by Acadians from Nova Scotia and later by Americans from Boston. Thomas Hancock (brother of Declaration of Independence signer John Hancock) also brought some horses to the island during the 18th century to await shipment to the Caribbean. When he died, the horses were left to their own devices.

Marooned but Not Forgotten

In 1801, Nova Scotia's government established a rescue station on Sable Island to help shipwreck survivors.

Officials also captured some of the island's horses and trained them for rescue operations. Whatever the weather—gales of hurricane strength, thick fog, blizzards—the horses would haul heavy rowboats across the island, tow lines through rolling seas to survivors, and transport wagonloads of people to shelters, sometimes across miles of sand dunes and through swamps.

Toward the end of the 19th century, Nova Scotia's government started holding annual roundups on the island and shipping horses to auctions in Halifax. Many became farm and buggy horses, and some were used as polo ponies, primarily because of their stamina. All the money earned from the auctions helped to finance the rescue station.

You're Not the Boss of Me!

As the horses became a valuable commodity, officials started trying to protect them. Winters on Sable Island were harsh and could decimate the herds, so the government built shelters and left feed out for the animals. But the horses remained independent. They weren't interested in the manmade structures and mostly ignored them. Instead, during the winter, they huddled—rumps to the wind—against the steep dunes. The feed didn't fare much better: the horses would defecate on it and then move elsewhere to paw through snow for familiar, but sparse, grass and weeds.

When the Nova Scotians introduced stallions from the mainland to strengthen the herd, the island stallions revolted. At least one mainland stallion ended up in quicksand and died. Others were injured. Men and horses could coexist on Sable Island, it seemed, but the horses didn't take kindly to interference.

The Island They Know

Today, 200 to 300 horses live on Sable Island. Winters are still hard, but summer transforms the area—freshwater ponds appear, and grass blankets small meadows and the shallows between dunes. The shaggy horses shed their thick winter hair and forage for dietary staples: grass, sandwort, reeds, and kelp washed ashore by storms. Family herds wander among hundreds of seals, and inquisitive foals sniff at the pups.

The Sable Island horses are small. Full-grown stallions rarely weigh more than 950 pounds; mares don't usually top 750 pounds. They are heavy-bodied and short-legged, reminiscent of Bretons, the favored horses of the early Acadians and probably the dominant bloodline.

Someone's Always Watching

Environment Canada, the country's conservation agency, protects the horses of Sable Island. They are no longer worked or auctioned, and by law, people cannot interfere with them. After 250 years of natural selection and little human interference, the Sable Island horses have become a distinct breed of their own. They are no longer Robinson Crusoes—they are successful colonizers who have adapted to an environment that still daunts men.

Singing Their Praises

*Test your horse-song savvy—name the artist
and the tune in each description.*

1. The protagonist rides horseback through a desert observing birds, insects, and a dry riverbed.

2. A Nebraska girl chases her runaway horse through a blizzard.

3. A baby drifts off to sleep dreaming of dapples and bays, with the promise of seeing dancing horses in the morning.

4. The narrator catches a wild horse and rides her along a steep ridge but then plunges over the side of the cliff after a snake spooks the horse.

5. A dreamer refuses to let his spirit be broken and imagines flying with horses in a "race with the wind."

6. A drifter runs from

the wrath of his girlfriend's father, duels with a gambler, and then returns home to find his girlfriend riding a mare.

7. A cowboy repeatedly chooses his love for horses over his love for Diane and can't keep his promise to quit the rodeo.

8. A colt born in western Kentucky spends lazy mornings running through green pastures, awaiting his destiny as a champion racehorse.

For answers, turn to page 223.

* * *

On Guard!

Whether they live in the wild or on farms, horses in a herd usually take turns acting as guards. Small groups have just one guard horse, but large herds (12 or more) often have two or three on duty at a time. The guards remain standing and alert while the other horses in the herd graze or relax. Each horse stands guard for about 30 minutes. When his "shift" is over, he'll lie down (or just return to grazing), and another horse will take his place.

More Believe It
or Not

On page 67, we started our list of the myth-information (and some truths) floating around about horses. Here are a few more.

Horses communicate mainly through neighs and whinnies.

Myth. This false perception is based on TV and movies in which horses converse using long sets of squeals and whinnies. In reality, horses are relatively quiet. Although they do sometimes "talk," body language (using their ears, nostrils, and eyes) is their main mode of communication. Should a horse flare his nostrils and lay his ears back, for example, you know to stand clear.

Some horses can go for days without food or water.

Fact. Throughout history, tribesmen and conquerors, including Alexander the Great, valued Akhal-Teke horses for their stamina and speed. Originally bred in the harsh desert of modern-day Turkmenistan, Akhal-Teke horses can withstand extreme temperatures and subsist for days on little food or water. When supplies are scarce, they survive on pellets of alfalfa and barley mixed with mutton fat.

Remarkably, 28 Akhal-Teke horses traveled 215 miles across Asia's Kara-Kum desert in 1935 without drinking any water. Today, the Turkmen are so proud of this horse that it is the centerpiece of Turkmenistan's state emblem.

Horses are as smart as human toddlers.

Fact . . . if we're talking math skills. British researchers have discovered that horses can count and have roughly the same mathematical skills as 10-month-old children do. In the study, horses kept track of the number of plastic apples placed into buckets and tended to choose the buckets that contained more apples. "The study absolutely proves that horses are more intelligent than people think," says lead researcher Claudia Uller.

Horses can't ride in cars or paint.

Myth. A remarkably humanlike pony named Patches is featured in a YouTube video with his two human roommates, brothers Robert and Herbert Thompson. As the video reveals, the white pony rides in cars, sits on the couch, fetches beer from the fridge, picks up the phone, and tucks himself into the queen-sized bed where he sleeps. When fun time comes, Patches loves to watch TV (his favorite genre is the Western . . . of course), eat cheeseburgers, and drink apple juice.

There's also an artistic mustang/quarter horse named Cholla who paints masterpieces holding brushes in his teeth. Like Vincent van Gogh, Cholla realized his drawing and painting abilities relatively late in life (at 19 years old). Four years later, his splashy watercolors have been displayed in more art galleries and exhibits than many human artists hope for. His owner, Renee Chambers, donates some originals to animal fund-raisers and sells others for thousands of dollars.

* * *

Grab a Spot on the Carousel

In the 1100s, carousels were training tools for Turkish and Arabian cavalries. The Spanish who first observed the maneuvers named the practice *carosella*, which means "little war." The early carosellas involved riders in baskets suspended from poles, fighting mock battles, and a game in which mounted soldiers speared rings attached to trees.

Carousels came to Europe soon after and continued to be used as training devices until the 1800s, when craftsmen reimagined them as a way to entertain. The carousel as we know it today—with carved horses on a rotating platform—took shape in Europe in the mid-19th century. In 1860, German carousel-maker Michael Dentzel sent his son Gustav to Philadelphia to test out the ride on Americans. They loved it, and the Dentzels set up a carousel-manufacturing plant in nearby Germantown. Today, Dentzel carousels are prized works of art, and many are still functioning; one of the most famous is at the San Francisco Zoo.

For the Record

*From the stable to the track, horses have
posted some amazing records.*

Biggest and Heaviest Horse: Samson

Born in England in 1846, Samson was a shire gelding.
Shires are known for being the tallest horse breed; on
average, they grow to be about 17 hands. Samson stood an
incredible 21.25 hands tall and weighed 3,360 pounds.

Smallest: Thumbelina

Guinness World Records made this record official in 2006
when it recognized the 17½-inch-tall miniature horse,
Thumbelina. Five years old at the time, "Thumby" was so
small that she spent more time with her owners' dogs than
with their other horses. In fact, she still usually sleeps with
the dogs in the barn.

Oldest: Old Billy

Born in England in 1760, Old Billy lived for 62 years.

Richest: Cigar

Since he started racing in 1993, Cigar has earned nearly
$10 million, taking home $4 million at the 1997 Dubai
World Cup alone. He's the great-grandson of Northern

Dancer (the first Canadian horse to win the Kentucky Derby) and the grandson of Seattle Slew (who won the Triple Crown in 1977). Cigar was born in 1990 in Maryland and won 16 straight races in 1995 and 1996, the first American horse to do so since 1950.

Fastest Racehorse: Big Racked and Onion Roll

A tie for the title. Both horses posted a speed of 43.26 mph on a quarter-mile track. (Big Racked in 1945 and Onion Roll in 1993.)

Longest Jump: Something

In South Africa in 1975, Something (and his trainer, Andre Ferreira) jumped 27 feet, 6¾ inches over water.

Highest Jump: Faithful

A onetime Chilean racehorse, Faithful retired in 1944 and started training at the country's cavalry school. He showed a lot of potential as a jumper and often went up against another horse at the school, Chileno. The two traded wins until 1948, when Faithful posted a jump of

7¾ feet and broke the South American record (which Chileno held until then). The time had come for a jump-off.

In February 1949, Faithful (now called Huaso, "cowboy" in Chilean) and Chileno were all set to duke it out. Chileno went first . . . barreling toward the 8-foot jump. But he crashed into it and never left the ground. Huaso went next. It took him three tries: first, he stopped short of the jump; second, he touched the fence; third, he sailed right over it.

* * *

Here Comes the Cavalry

In the Middle Ages, cavalries were the preferred method of fighting in Europe. But long before gallant knights climbed onto their trusty steeds, the ancient Greeks hitched horses to chariots and drove them in battle.

One of the earliest literary mentions of using horses for military service comes from Homer's *Iliad*, written around 800 BC. Homer includes several stories of warriors driving two-horse chariots to the battlefield and then dismounting to fight with swords and spears. Why not just fight on horseback? Greek horses at the time were too small to ride. That didn't come until about 400 BC, when the Greeks had bred horses large enough to support a man's weight. They took those animals to war and managed to defeat a group of Persian invaders.

Horses Are Therapists, Too

Imagine a loving, nonjudgmental therapist who helps those suffering from cerebral palsy, Down syndrome, or autism. Throw in an ability to ease the awkwardness of troubled youngsters, and that therapist might easily be called a miracle worker—or a horse.

History, Horses, and Healing

The combination of horses and healing was first noted more than two millennia ago in ancient Greece. The Greeks believed that horseback riding could help put into balance the "four humors" (blood, phlegm, yellow bile, and black bile) of people suffering from illness. Injured soldiers also rode horses to improve their health. In the 17th century, the "riding cure" surfaced again when English doctors prescribed it for gout. But it was Cassaign, an 18th-century French doctor, who first wrote that horseback riding could improve neurological disorders because it helped with posture, balance, joint movement, and psychological well-being . . . a finding that modern therapists confirm.

Horse therapy gained international attention in 1952 when Denmark's Lis Hartel won an Olympic silver medal for dressage. Her win stunned the world because eight years earlier, Hartel had been stricken with polio. Her arm, leg, and thigh muscles had been affected, but Hartel, already an accomplished equestrian, was determined to ride again. With the help of supervised riding sessions, she improved her muscle strength and coordination. And even though by 1952 she still needed crutches to walk, she became a world-class riding competitor—and the first woman to win an Olympic equestrian medal. Hartel always insisted that riding improved her health, and doctors took note. Soon after her victories, therapeutic riding programs sprang up in Europe, North America, and Australia.

Healthy with a Horse

Today, there are hundreds of therapeutic and social programs involving horses. They generally cost about $100 for one session, which usually lasts for 30 minutes to an hour, and they offer benefits to people with all types of disabilities. A physically disabled person can improve balance, strength, and agility. A mentally disabled rider experiences improved sensory processing, focus, and concentration. A socially troubled rider develops a sense of responsibility and self-confidence. And for all three groups, the therapies are also a lot of fun.

There are three primary types of riding therapy:

- Therapeutic riding is supervised recreational riding for people with disabilities.
- Hippotherapy (*hippo* is Greek for horse) is more structured. It involves a trained professional who assists the patient on horseback—the motions and experience of riding are used as a therapy.

- A third program is equine psychotherapy for behavioral, social, and emotional growth. In this program, communicating and caring for the animal are key parts of the therapy.

Gaining Skills and Confidence

Some centers specialize in one particular type of program, while others integrate aspects of all three. A typical therapeutic riding lesson for a child with autism or Down syndrome might last an hour, with lessons in grooming and tack, mounting, dismounting, and riding. The first sessions might consist of gentle lessons like patting the horse or holding the reins, but as the children become more comfortable and learn more about the animal, they will develop independent equestrian skills. Eventually, the riders may even enter special horse shows and competitions, which also boost confidence and self-esteem.

Hippotherapy is often used specifically for children with physical problems like cerebral palsy. These sessions usually last about 30 minutes, while the therapist controls the horse's movement and the patient sits on a riding pad rather than a saddle to better feel what the horse is doing. The horse's body warmth combined with the rhythm of his movement promotes relaxation and reduces muscle tension. This allows the child to adjust his posture to the movement of the horse and remain upright. Some children with physical disabilities have even learned to walk during hippotherapy sessions.

During an equine psychotherapy program, each participant is assigned a horse. The children learn riding skills and the challenges of caring for a 1,000-pound animal. The program teaches the value of patience, focus, and commitment. A study showed that one group of teenagers who participated in equine psychotherapy programs became less aggressive, angry, and suicidal.

From the Horse's Point of View

Not just any horse can be a therapist. Hippotherapy, for example, requires horses who can vary their strides as needed. Therapeutic riding horses also need to be flexible, move forward freely, and respond well to voice commands. In general, horses used for therapy can be of nearly any type or breed, but they must have good manners and a gentle disposition. (Stallions rarely make the cut.)

And how does the job affect the animals? In a study of 28 horses (who comprised 15 different breeds), veterinarians used behavior studies and cortisol levels to measure stress in horses working in equine-assisted therapy. Eighty-two percent of the horses had lower cortisol levels (meaning they were less stressed) after working in therapy programs than average working horses. Even for these "miracle therapists," there seems to be a benefit to the work.

*   *   *

Watch out! Horses can kick backward, forward, and sideways (called "cow-kicking").

Equine Intelligence

*Horse lovers know that equines are among
the smartest animals around.*

"Horse sense is the thing a horse has which keeps it from
betting on people."

—*W. C. Fields*

"There will never be a time when the old horse is not
superior to any auto ever made."

—*Will Rogers*

"He knows when you're happy, he knows when you're
comfortable, he knows when you're confident, and he
always knows when you have carrots."

—*Anonymous*

"When I hear somebody talking about a horse being
stupid, I figure it's a sure sign that it has outfoxed them."

—*Tom Dorance, trainer*

"They say princes learn no art truly but the art of horsemanship. The reason is, the brave beast is no flatterer. He
will throw a prince as soon as his groom."

—*Ben Jonson, Renaissance playwright*

Off to the Races:
Citation and Ruffian

Get ready to ride two more horses who made racing history.

Citation: The Equine Millionaire

Citation was never meant to be an ordinary horse. In 1941, Warren Wright—the Calumet Baking Powder heir who owned Calumet Farms in Lexington, Kentucky—wanted to breed a great Thoroughbred racer. So he bought Hydroplane II, the daughter of English champions, to mate with his stud horse, Bull Lea. Moving Hydroplane from England to the United States was tricky because Nazi U-boats were sinking ships in the Atlantic. But Wright wasn't dissuaded: he brought her via the Pacific to San Francisco, and from there, she traveled across the country to Kentucky. On April 11, 1945, Hydroplane produced a bay foal named Citation.

In 1947, two-year-old Citation ran his first race—and won by half a length. At his second race, he broke the Arlington Park record for five furlongs (five-eighths of a mile). That year, Citation raced nine times and racked up eight victories. (His only loss came to Bewitched, his stablemate. Their trainer had said that whoever led going into the stretch should win, and Bewitched was there.)

But 1948 turned out to be Citation's big year. In his first and second races as a three-year-old, he easily beat Armed, 1947's Horse of the Year. In all, he won 19 of 20 races that year—the single loss (second place) was with a new jockey, Eddie Arcardo (after Citation's original jockey, Al Snider, died in an accident). The horse easily swept the 1948 Triple Crown, becoming the first to win all three major races in 25 years, and he was voted 1948's Horse of the Year.

Osteoarthritis kept Citation off the track until January 1950, but when he came back, it was with a major win. He took top place at Santa Anita—his 16th win in a row, a record for North American stakes horses that lasted 46 years. Citation also won the Golden Gate Mile, setting a world record of 1:33.6, which stood until 1966. But the now-five-year-old struggled with injuries and lost seven close races that season. Still, he remained in competition because Wright's dying wish was that Citation be the first horse to win $1 million in race purses. In 1951, after losing his first four races, Citation took to the track three more times, winning the Century Handicap, American Handicap, and Hollywood Gold Cup and fulfilling Wright's wish. Citation also earned a well-deserved retirement, entry into the racing hall of fame, and a third-place ranking in *Blood-Horse* magazine's top 100 horses of the 20th century (behind Man o' War and Secretariat).

Ruffian: Lady of the Track

Born April 17, 1972, near Paris, Kentucky, Ruffian was a

big, dark bay. She won her first race by 15 lengths and set a track record. In 1974, she won the Eclipse Award for Outstanding Two-Year-Old Filly and earned the nickname "Queen of the Fillies." The only ominous note was a hairline fracture that ended her undefeated season that year.

But Ruffian returned to racing in 1975 and picked up her winning streak right where she'd left off. She won the three races that made up the Filly Triple Crown: the Acorn, Mother Goose, and Coaching Club American Oaks. One Ruffian admirer told the press that "she may even be better than Secretariat." (Since the admirer was Secretariat's trainer, Lucien Laurin, the quote made headlines.)

Ruffian had beaten the best female horses of her generation, so a clamor went up for a match race with a champion colt. In July 1975 at Belmont Park, Ruffian took on Foolish Pleasure, the undefeated colt who'd won the Kentucky Derby. Billed as a "battle of the sexes," the race attracted millions of television viewers. Ruffian led for a quarter mile, but then tragedy struck. Her right foreleg broke, and it took her jockey 50 yards to finally stop her from running— she was that determined to stay in the lead.

A team of top veterinarians was unable to save Ruffian, and after three hours of surgery, she was euthanized. Millions of stunned fans mourned her death, and no match races have been held at Belmont since. The public outcry over her death also was the catalyst for several innovations in the treatment of injured horses. These included better medications and the "recovery pool"—a vat of warm water in which horses can recover from anesthesia after surgery without re-injuring themselves.

In spite of the tragedy, Ruffian remains the "Queen of the Fillies." And *Sports Illustrated* has ranked her as one of the greatest female athletes, human or nonhuman, of the 20th century.

To read about the Godolphin Arabian and Eclipse, turn to page 58. For Man o' War and Secretariat, turn to page 39.

* * *

Funnyman

Comedian Chevy Chase's grandfather, Edward L. Chase, was a renowned equestrian artist whose studio included an entire horse skeleton. So you might say that Chevy grew up around horses. (Edward also wrote and illustrated an equine guide called *The Big Book of Horses*.) Today, Chevy's whole family rides, and they own a pair of Icelandic horses with unpronounceable names, so the family simply calls them "Bob and Candy."

The Wildest Show
Behind Bars

*At one time, Huntsville's Texas Prison Rodeo was
the place to be for the state's wildest rodeo action.*

In 1894, Marshall Lee Simmons was about to graduate
from the University of Texas and start work at his
brother's law firm when he was arrested for shooting a man
who had bad-mouthed one of his relatives. The shooting
was ruled self-defense, and Simmons went on to become a
businessman, banker, sheriff, and eventually general man-
ager of the state prison system.

It was in this capacity that he came up with the idea of
having a rodeo for prisoners in Huntsville. He billed it as
"the fastest and wildest rodeo," and even though Marshall
Lee Simmons retired in 1936, his rodeo—which earned the
nickname "the Wildest Show Behind Bars"—rode on for
another 50 years.

Jailhouse Rodeo

Simmons's Texas Prison Rodeo started out as a way for the
inmates and staff to have a little fun. The Depression was
in full swing, and the people of Huntsville needed some
entertainment. Plus, the prisoners were often clamoring

149

for something to do. Bullriding, calfroping, wild horse racing, and bronco busting seemed like the perfect solution.

The prison usually held the rodeo on Sunday afternoons—occasional weekday shows were added—in a baseball field near the Walls Unit (Huntsville's death row). Inmates from all of the area prisons were welcome as long as they had a record of good behavior. In fact, any inmate who kept his nose clean for a year was eligible.

Hustle and Bustle

By 1933, the audience was 15,000 strong, and it continued to grow, sometimes doubling from year to year. Soon the prison needed to build wooden benches to hold all the spectators. The rodeo also brought lots of business to Huntsville: even retail shops and restaurants stayed open at a time when most places closed on Sundays.

The guards were paid for overtime, and the prisoners got to see the fruits of their labor—not just all that rodeo practice, but the planning and preparation work as well. The wild cattle the farm prisoners rounded up for the event were finally put to work, the uniforms sewn by women prisoners stretched across the backs of the bull riders, and a midway full of prison-made arts and crafts found a market.

Big Time in the Big House

As word caught on about the rodeo—so much so that people had to be turned away at the gate—the wooden bleachers were replaced by a concrete megastructure. Over the years, the rodeo had invented its own unusual tongue-in-cheek events, like "Hard Money," where convicts in red shirts tried to remove a sack of cash from between a bull's horns, or the greased pig contest in which female prisoners tried to put greased pigs in a sack. By the mid-1980s, the event was grossing almost half a million dollars, all of which was used to help run the prison.

The lineup also included exhibitions by the top rodeo stars from around the country and entertainment courtesy of the likes of Willie Nelson and Loretta Lynn. By then, the rodeo was attracting 100,000 people a year.

Adios, Cowboys!

For more than 50 years, the Texas Prison Rodeo was a popular local tradition. But in 1986, engineers declared the prison's rodeo facility unfit to safely hold the massive crowds. The prison couldn't afford to pay for the necessary reconstructions, so the Texas Prison Rodeo closed for good.

Lots of Texans have lobbied to bring it back, but as Dan Beto, director of the Sam Houston State University Correctional Management Institute of Texas, told the *Houston Chronicle*: "When we had a prison rodeo, we had a lot of inmates who had some agricultural background . . . Most of the inmates who come to the prison system now are from major metropolitan areas. You're dealing with a different kind of inmate, a different culture, a different time."

So You Want to Be a Jockey?

Want to don the silks and mount a winner at the starting gate? Well, before you quit your day job, read about what it takes to make a career as a jockey.

Q: How old do you have to be to start working as a jockey?
A: Most states allow jockeys to work as young as 16, as long as they have parental permission.

Q: How much can jockeys weigh?
A: There's no international standard, and limits vary by state and track. But in general, first-year jockeys weigh 102 to 105 pounds, and experienced jockeys don't exceed 113 pounds.

Q: What kind of training do you need?
A: Although there's no set career path for jockeys, most start out working in stables, walking or grooming horses. Then they work up to exercising horses during workouts and advance to jobs as apprentice jockeys. Along the way, of course, they must acquire exceptional riding skills. Eddie Arcaro, who won more than 4,700 races and is the only rider to have won the Triple Crown twice, started out

at 15 as an exercise boy. He soon became an apprentice to several experienced riders, and he won his first race after working at the racetracks for just two years.

At the apprentice stage, riders get an apprentice license. When they've had that for at least a year, they can apply at almost any racetrack to get a full jockey license, which is required to run in all professional races.

Q: *How does a jockey earn money?*
A: For each race, jockeys earn mount fees (ranging from $25 for a low-profile race to $100 for a big race like the Kentucky Derby). But the real money comes from taking home a percentage of the race purse . . . though that means you've got to win, place, or show. Most jockeys earn between $25,000 and $30,000 per year. Superstar jockeys, though, can earn millions of dollars, and the top 100 jockeys in the world—like Garrett Gomez and Rafael Bejarano—average about $6 million a year.

Q: *How likely is it a jockey will be injured on the job?*
A: Horseracing is one of the most dangerous sports in the world—jockeys have a 5 percent chance of getting seriously injured each time they ride. (Compare

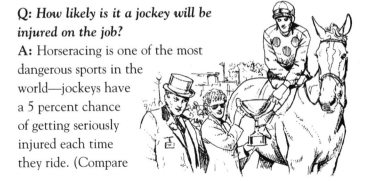

that to NASCAR racing, where drivers have about a 0.25 percent chance of getting into a serious accident.)

Q: For how many years can a jockey ride?
A: There is no age limit.

Q: What is the Jockeys' Guild?
A: The Jockeys' Guild is the union that protects professional jockeys. Its original purpose was to improve the working conditions for jockeys, especially by offering health insurance and survivor benefits for the families of jockeys who are killed on the job. Eddie Arcaro, Sam Renick, Lester Haas, and others founded the union in 1940. In late 2007, the Jockeys' Guild filed for bankruptcy as a result of the rising costs of its health insurance plan and decreased income from racetrack associations. But financial reorganization is underway, and the racing community is committed to keeping the organization intact.

Q: What are the guild's membership requirements?
A: To be a member in good standing in the Jockeys' Guild, riders must have a valid jockey license, comply with the regulations of all racing jurisdictions, have ridden 100 mounts in the previous or current calendar year, and pay membership dues. Jockeys aren't required to join the union to ride, but because membership is the only way to receive benefits, most of them do join.

Military Mounts

These two horses were war heroes.

Babieca Saves Spain

Rodrigo Díaz de Vivar, better known as El Cid ("the Lord"), was an 11th-century Spanish military hero who always led his armies from the back of his white Andalusian horse, Babieca. There are two legends offering theories for how El Cid got Babieca:

- El Cid's godfather gave the young man the pick of any horse in his herd, and El Cid chose a white stallion whom his godfather thought was the weakest of the bunch. In response, the godfather muttered, "*Babieca, babieca,*" which means "stupid" in Spanish.

- The second story paints Babieca as one of the Spanish king's best horses. When a mounted knight challenged El Cid to a duel, the king gave him the white stallion to ensure that the fight was fair.

Either way, El Cid and Babieca were inseparable. They were already legendary when the warrior led his army into one last battle against the Moors for control of Valencia in southern Spain. El Cid actually died before the battle— he'd been wounded in a skirmish outside the city's walls and passed away just before the siege at Valencia. But his

155

followers tied his corpse upright in his saddle and put a sword in his hand, and Babieca carried El Cid into the fray, inspiring the Spaniards and panicking the Moors, who believed El Cid has risen from the dead. Thus, the Spanish kingdom was saved.

Onward, Rienzi!

In 1864, Confederates attacked Union general Phillip Sheridan's troops in Virginia's Shenandoah Valley. Sheridan was about 12 miles away at the time, attending a meeting in the town of Winchester. But when he got word that his men were under siege, he jumped on his horse Rienzi, who galloped across the war-torn countryside and delivered Sheridan to the battlefield. Once there, the general orchestrated a successful Union counterattack against Confederate troops, a victory considered by many historians to be a crucial turning point in the war.

Shenandoah was his most famous effort, but in all, Rienzi saw service in 19 battles and sustained several wounds. His efforts earned him a lasting tribute when he died in 1878: Rienzi was stuffed and put on display—first at a U.S. Army museum in New York City (it burned down in 1922) and then at the Smithsonian Institution's Hall of Armed Forces History, where he remains today. Reinzi also got a name change. After the horse's heroics at Shenandoah, Sheridan renamed him Winchester.

More military mounts on page 202.

Who's Got Mail?

*"Wanted: Young, skinny, wiry fellows . . . Must be expert
riders. Willing to risk death daily. Orphans preferred."
Get ready to ride the Pony Express—by the numbers.*

1
Mail deliveries lost during the 18 months the Pony
Express existed (April 1860 to October 1861).

3
Partners who founded the Pony Express: William Russell,
William Waddell, and Alexander Majors. They wanted to
reduce the amount of time it took to get mail across the
expanding United States; the fastest route before the
Express took 24 days. The Pony Express averaged 10 days
in the summer and 12 to 16 days during the winter.

$5
Initial price to mail a letter via the Pony Express. By July
1861, it had dropped to $1.

6
Besides the mail, items a rider usually took with him: a water
bottle, a Bible, a knife, a revolver, some other type of gun,
and a horn to alert station masters that he was coming.

9 days (and 23 hours)

Length of time it took for the first Pony Express run to travel from St. Joseph, Missouri, to Sacramento, California. The riders carried 49 letters and five telegrams. When the final rider arrived in California on April 13, 1860, the *New York Times* reported that "citizens paraded the streets with bands of music, fireworks were set off . . . the best feeling was manifested by everybody." The fastest ride was seven days and 17 hours in 1860 for a ride that brought President Abraham Lincoln's inaugural address to the West Coast.

11 years

Age of the youngest Pony Express rider. The oldest was in his 40s. Most were about 20.

$100

A rider's pay per month, on average.

125 pounds

Maximum weight for a Pony Express rider.

200

Number of relay stations along the route. The stations were set up 10 miles apart because that's about how far the horses could travel at a full gallop without stopping. At every station, a rider would pick up a new horse. Every 75 to 100 miles, a new rider would take over.

400+
Number of horses that the Pony Express used. Each one weighed less than 900 pounds and stood around 14½ hands tall.

1860
Year Congress authorized money to build a telegraph line between Missouri and California to connect the eastern United States with its new western settlements. It took 17 months to build, and it was the completion of the telegraph in October 1861 that put the Pony Express out of business.

1,966 miles
Distance between St. Joseph, Missouri, and Sacramento, California.

$200,000
Amount of money the owners lost on the Pony Express. They invested about $700,000 initially and expected to get a subsidy from the U.S. government to cover some of their expenses. But when the Civil War broke out in 1861, that money was no longer available, and when they sold the operation in 1861, they had to take a loss.

Conquer with the Mongols

Here's one vacation just for horse lovers.

Some of history's greatest horsemen rode on the barren steppes of Mongolia. The 13th-century troops who served under Genghis Khan were skilled riders who traveled all over Asia, capturing everything along the way. In just 250 years, these mounted warriors conquered more people and a larger area than the Romans did in four centuries. By the time of Genghis Khan's death in 1227, his empire stretched from Beijing, China, to the Afghan border, from Siberia to the border of Tibet, and through Turkey and into Europe.

Horse Play

Mongolia is still one of the world's most horse-dependent cultures, but its people are now famous for their peaceful and welcoming hospitality. But intrepid travelers know that it's still possible to witness—and even experience—the life of a warrior for the mighty khan. A British company called High and Wild sponsors a Mongolian adventure that begins when visitors arrive in Ulaanbataar (Mongolia's capital) and trade their Western garb for traditional Mongolian warrior robes. Then it's on to warrior training camp in the Gobi Desert grasslands, where visitors ride small, fast Mongolian horses and learn the horsemanship, discipline, and battle tactics that made Genghis Khan's warriors the greatest of their day. At night they guard the herds as Mongol warriors once did and even learn to sing ancient Mongolian camp songs and drink an alcoholic beverage made from fermented mares' milk.

* * *

The English Triple Crown

England has its own Triple Crown, and the term actually originated there in 1853, when a horse named West Australian won the country's three major races. Like the American version, the English Triple Crown includes only three-year-old Thoroughbreds, and it's as hard to win the title in England as it is in the United States. Only 15 horses have done it, the last in 1970. The races are . . .

- The 2,000 Guineas Stakes: First run in 1809. This one-mile race occurs in late April or early May at Newmarket Racecourse in Suffolk.

- The Epsom Derby: First run in 1780. This race is one mile, four furlongs, and 10 yards long. It's run the first weekend in June at Epsom Downs Racecourse in Surrey.

- The St. Leger Stakes: First run in 1776. Every September at Town Moor in Yorkshire, horses gather to compete in this race, which is one mile, six furlongs, and 132 yards long.

They're Ponylicious

Toys like the Cabbage Patch Kids and Tickle Me, Elmo are no match for My Little Pony.

- First introduced by toy manufacturer Hasbro in 1982, My Little Pony (MLP) has three generations of fans. The toys were discontinued in the late 1980s because of waning sales, but were reintroduced in 1997 and 2003.

- At the peak of the MLP craze (the mid-1980s), the ponies were more profitable than Barbie.

- Collectors differentiate the generations of MLP as G-1, G-2, and G-3. The first ponies introduced in the G-1 line were Blossom, Blue Bell, Butterscotch, Cotton Candy, Minty, and Snuzzle. These ponies looked the most like real horses—despite the rainbow colors.

- The four most common MLP names: Ember, Cuddles, Sniffles, and Snookums.

- MLP accessories are available to suit many activities. There are bumper cars; wedding veils, engagement rings, and garters; lipstick and hoof polish; boom boxes and Walkmen; rollerskates, tennis rackets, and skis; and tea sets.

- The toys inspired one feature-length animated movie, two television series, and seven straight-to-video movies.

- A stage performance featuring live-action versions of MLPs toured the country between 2006 and 2008. Billed as the "World's Largest Tea Party," the show included songs like "Positively Pink" and "Shake Your Cutie" (sung to the tune of "Shake Your Booty").

- Fans of the ponies can join the MLP Birthday Club. Benefits include an e-mail birthday greeting from the ponies and a newsletter filled with party ideas ("Pin the Tiara on the Pony") and party recipes ("Sparkleworks Silly-Face Pizza" and "Cotton Candy Funfetti Unicorn Horns").

- Since 2004, collectors from around the world have gathered to trade ponies at a two-day annual convention called the My Little Pony Fair. Workshops teach fans how to customize and restore ponies . . . like how to "re-hair" manes and tails and how to spot "fakies" (counterfeit MLPs).

Horsey Humor

The good, the bad, and the horsey.

"A horse is dangerous at both ends and uncomfortable in the middle."

—*Ian Fleming*

"To err is human, to whinny equine."

—*Cheryl Farner, horse trainer*

"They used to take your horse, and if they were caught they got hung for it. Now if they take your car and they are caught, it's a miracle."

—*Will Rogers*

"Fight smog, buy a horse."

—*Charlette Moore, writer*

"If you're a cowboy and you're dragging a guy behind your horse, I bet it would really make you mad if you looked back and the guy was reading a magazine."

—*Jack Handey*

"One of the worst things that can happen in life is to win a bet on a horse at an early age."

—*Danny McGoorty, Irish pool player*

Canada's Royal Horsemen

The Royal Canadian Mounted Police force's Musical Ride is a colorful exhibition of precision horsemanship. And it's become one of Canada's most recognizable institutions.

Mounted Is No Misnomer

The Mounties formed in 1874 as Canada's national police force and were mostly charged with the task of keeping order on the country's expanding western frontier. Over the years, their role evolved to include protecting national and international dignitaries, enforcing federal laws, and policing rural areas. Today, more than 24,000 Mounties make up the force.

Since the beginning, the Mounties' work and image have been associated with horses. In fact, until 1966, equitation training was mandatory for all new recruits. Each was assigned a horse and saddle right along with the uniform and handcuffs.

Setting It All to Music

The Mounties' Musical Ride is a colorful, precision performance of 36 men on horseback. The riders wear traditional Mountie uniforms (red coats and wide-brimmed Stetsons), and they execute a variety of cavalry maneuvers. The techniques date back to the 1700s and the days of Prussia's Frederick the Great. Later, other European countries adopted them. And since so many of the riders who worked with the original Mounties had roots in Great Britain and had been trained in the British tradition, it was only natural that they'd integrate that training into their group's displays. At the turn of the 20th century, the Mounties decided to show off their training to the public, and those maneuvers were choreographed to music. The first official public Musical Ride took place in 1901.

The Mounties were excellent horsemen, but adding music did teach them a hard lesson or two along the way. Initially, they experimented with bands on horseback, but as soon as the instruments sounded, the musicians' horses spooked. At one exhibition at RCMP Headquarters in Regina, Saskatchewan, the horses threw their musical riders and bolted at the first trumpet blare. By the time the Mounties rounded up all the animals, several had run as many as 40 miles. From then on, the band stood apart from the horses—and remained on the ground.

Now That's Entertainment

The Musical Ride has become a well-known event, both in Canada and abroad, and with the exception of the World War I and World War II years, it has an uninterrupted history.

The first international event was in 1902, when the Musical Ride traveled to England to represent Canada at the coronation of King Edward VII. In 1937, the Musical

Ride packed New York's Madison Square Garden and, two years later, was back in the Big Apple to perform at the World's Fair. And it's still going strong—in 2008, the Musical Ride traveled to several American venues, including the Vermont State Fair and the Pennsylvania National Horse Show.

Getting Ready for the Ride

Thoroughbreds and Hanoverians are the standard breeds used for the Ride. The RCMP has even set up its own in-house breeding program. The horses selected for the Musical Ride are always black, weigh 1,000 to 1,400 pounds, and stand 16 to 17 hands.

The breeding farm and year-round training facility are just a few miles from Ottawa, Canada's capital city and the site of RCMP Headquarters. The horses spend three years there before moving to the training stables. Another two and a half years elapse before a horse is ready for the Ride.

During those years, the horses learn everything from traditional commands to the intricate Musical Ride formations. Another important part of the training process involves getting the horses accustomed to performing in front of large crowds. The arenas and stadiums where the riders perform can be loud, chaotic, and distracting for animals who spook easily.

Charge!

The Mounties who participate in the Musical Ride perform

several maneuvers during the show, but the two most famous are the Dome and the Charge.

- **Dome:** The horses form a circle and face the center, while the riders hold their lances up, forming a dome shape in the center of the circle. This formation is so famous that it used to appear on the back of Canada's $50 bill.
- **Charge:** The most exciting part of the Musical Ride, this maneuver requires the riders to lower their lances while their horses gallop at full speed.

On the Road

Today, the Musical Ride carries out about 50 performances during its annual summer tour. Riders also perform in parades and other special occasions. Thirty-six horses and horsemen—33 for the Ride and three alternates—travel to events all over the world. Some of these are for charitable causes and raise more than $1 million annually.

* * *

Home Again

In prehistoric times, horses roamed across North America, but about 12,000 years ago, the animals went extinct there. Fortunately, about a million years before, many of them had migrated to Asia across the Bering Land Bridge. That kept the species alive, and horses finally returned to North America in the 15th century with European explorers.

The Lucky Horseshoe

*Iron has long been thought to possess magical powers, and
blacksmiths were often considered sorcerers, partly because of
a long-held belief that fire could repel demons. So it's no
wonder the horseshoe became a symbol of good luck.*

A Deal with the Devil

The horseshoe legend began with this story: The devil (in
disguise) visited St. Dunstan, a 10th-century English
blacksmith. Despite the disguise, Dunstan recognized the
devil, nailed him to a wall, and began shoeing his cloven
hooves until the devil begged for mercy. Dunstan released
him only after the devil promised never to enter a home
where a horseshoe hung over the door.

Horseshoe Need to Know

- In the United States, the common belief is that a horseshoe should be hung with the points up—to keep the
  luck from spilling out. But in most of
  Europe (except parts of Ireland and
  Britain), people hang their protective
  horseshoes facing downward—so the
  luck pours onto the household's
  residents and visitors.
- The luckiest horseshoe is one off the hind

leg of a large gray mare—unless you consider gray horses to be bad luck.

- Supposedly, horseshoes also have the power to turn away witches, cure hiccups, and protect against the evil eye.

- A circular ring made from an iron horseshoe nail gives the same protection against evil as the horseshoe itself. Ancient cultures like the Chaldeans and Egyptians used similar ring-shaped charms (in the form of a serpent biting its own tail) to symbolize eternity.

* * *

More Horse Talk

"Horses make a landscape look beautiful." —*Alice Walker*

"Four things greater than all things are women and horses and power and war."
—*Rudyard Kipling*

"There is something about jumping a horse over a fence, something that makes you feel good. Perhaps it's the risk, the gamble. In any event, it's a thing I need."
—*William Faulkner*

"I can make a general in five minutes, but a good horse is hard to replace."
—*Abraham Lincoln*

Rockin' Horses

*We couldn't pass up a story that combined Genghis Khan,
Hannibal's elephants, the Nazi SS, General Patton, and
of course horses. They all come together for the tale
of Vienna's dancing Lipizzan stallions.*

Crisscross Breeding

Spain's Vilano horses were well known for their strength
as long ago as the days of Julius Caesar, and the horses carried Hannibal's warriors across the Alps (alongside those
famous elephants). Then someone thought to cross
Vilanos with the barb horses (whose ancestors may have
carried Genghis Khan and his hordes from Asia). The
result was the Andalusian.

In 1580, Charles (Karl), Archduke of Vienna, founded
a stud farm at Lipica (also called Lipizza), a village in
Slovenia close to the Italian border. There, using the
Spanish Andalusians, the archduke created strong, grace-
ful horses that are born dark but whose coats gradually
lighten to a brilliant, snowy white—the Lipizzan breed.

At about the same time, Austrian royalty founded the
Spanish Riding School in Vienna to teach classical
horsemanship. The school used and bred Lipizzans
exclusively.

Getting Their Kicks in Battle

By the 1600s, Lipizzans were a must-have for both the European aristocracy and the military. The horses were fast and strong, but it was their ability to leap and kick that made them essential battlefield companions.

Enemy ground troops feared the Lipizzans' powerful kicks—called "airs above the ground." These airs included a *courbette* (where horses reared on their hind legs and jumped) and a *croupade* (a leap that had the horses tuck their legs in midair). But the *capriole* was the most dazzling feat: a horse leapt with its forelegs drawn under its chest, and then, in midair, it kicked out violently with its hind legs.

The Performance of Their Lives

Over the next 300 years, the Lipizzans survived some famous assaults on Austria, including attacks by Napoleon's armies and World War I. It was World War II, though, that nearly defeated them. In 1945, Germany was losing the war, and the Allies were bombing Vienna. Hoping to save his horses, Colonel Alois Podhajsky, the director of the Spanish Riding School, relocated all of the stallions to St. Martin in upper Austria, 200 miles away. There, Podhajsky had the horses put on a performance for U.S. general George Patton, a horse lover and equestrian. (Patton even competed in the equestrian event in the 1912 Olympics.) Podhajsky asked Patton to make the stallions protected wards of the U.S. Army, and he eventually agreed.

Operation Cowboy

The mares, though, were still in danger. The Nazis had taken control of the Lipizzan mares and foals and moved them to a stud farm in Hostau, Czechoslovakia. An American soldier, Colonel Charles H. Reed of the Second Cavalry Brigade, was looking for Allied prisoners held at Hostau when he learned of the horses' whereabouts. (The information came from a captured German general who worried that the Soviet troops might destroy the Lipizzans or ship them to the Soviet Union.) Thus began "Operation Cowboy," the American army's effort to save the Lipizzans and liberate Hostau.

On April 28, 1945, the Americans entered the town, and according to Reed, it was a "fiesta," rather than a battle. Allied prisoners lined the streets, and surrendering German troops welcomed the American soldiers with salutes and an honor guard. As for the horses, 375 Lipizzans were rescued—as well as 100 Arabians, 200 Thoroughbreds, and 600 Russian horses. The U.S. Army protected all of them when Nazi troops attacked Hostau one last time. But by May 7, the war in Europe was over, and arrangements were made to return the Lipizzans to the Republic of Austria.

A Tall Tail?

Over the years, General Patton got credit for rescuing the Lipizzans. A 1963 Disney movie called *Miracle of the White Stallions* emphasized the St. Martin performance, and according to Col. Reed, Patton ordered the rescue of the mares in Czechoslovakia himself. But Patton maintained that he had little to do with the horses' rescue and even thought the display at St. Martin was odd. In his autobiography, Patton wrote,

> It struck me as rather strange that, in the midst of a world at war, some 20 young and middle-aged men in great physical condition . . . had spent their entire time teaching a group of horses to wiggle their butts and raise their feet . . . Much as I like horses, this seemed to me wasted energy.

No matter how it happened, though, it's thanks to the U.S. Second Cavalry that one of the best-known European horse breeds still performs at Austria's Spanish Riding School.

* * *

Fast Lipizzan Facts

- The Lipizzan is a long-lived horse—30 to 35 years is its average life span.

- Lipizzans are usually born black and, over a period of 6 to 10 years, slowly go gray until they turn pure white. Occasionally, Lipizzan foals are born white, but that doesn't happen often. (In the days of the Hapsburg dynasty, the white colts pulled royal vehicles.)

- Lipizzans are a rare breed. Today, there are only about 3,000 registered worldwide.

Horse Sense

*Think you know everything there is to know about horses in
entertainment and literature? Don't let our quiz throw you.*

1. This famous literary horse, who appears in his own
1871 fictional equine autobiography, was based on the
author's brother's horse, Bessie.

2. Mary O'Hara's 1941 children's novel about this beloved
horse was made into a popular 1950s television show and
more recently adapted into a 2006 movie starring country
singer Tim McGraw. (The horse's name means "little girl"
in Swedish.)

3. This palomino stallion began his film career by starring
with Errol Flynn in *The Adventures of Robin Hood* and Bob
Hope in *Son of Paleface*. He later found fame on the small
screen.

4. This pale quarter horse starred in Westerns alongside
his human sidekick, Dale Evans.

5. Elizabeth Taylor starred in 1945's *National Velvet*, the
story of a little girl who wins this horse in a lottery and
trains him for England's Grand National steeplechase.

6. This championship racehorse—a descendant of Man o' War—had some unusual friends at his barn: an older horse named Pumpkin, a dog named Pocatell, and a spider monkey named Jo-Jo all lived in his stall.

7. Radar O'Reilly gave this horse to his commanding officer, Colonel Potter, on the TV series *M*A*S*H*.

8. A 1947 novel tells the story of this real pony who was also immortalized when she put her hoofprints in the cement outside a local theater.

9. Walter Farley was just 26 in 1941 when he published his first book about this majestic horse who is stranded on a deserted island.

10. The Cisco Kid, focus of the 1950s television show of the same name, was based on a 1907 O. Henry story called "The Cabellero's Way." Played by actor Duncan Renaldo, the television Cisco wore a large sombrero, embroidered shirts, and silver spurs, and sat in the saddle of this black-and-white pinto.

11. Quintessential Western hero John Wayne starred with dozens of horses throughout his career, but his favorite was this chestnut stunt horse, his equine costar in the film *True Grit*.

For answers, turn to page 224.

Horsing Around the World

*Horse museums around the globe cater to equine
enthusiasts. Here are five of the best.*

The Living Horse Museum (France)

In 1719, Prince Louis IV Henri created one of the most
beautiful palaces in the world—for horses. Louis Henri
believed in reincarnation and thought that, after his
death, he would return as a horse. So he hired French
architect Jean Aubert to design the Grandes Ecuries (the
Grand Stables) at his castle in northern France. High ceilings, relief sculptures, and a monumental dome make the
large stable feel palatial: 623 feet long by 59 feet wide,
with walls 16 feet high. Once home to 240 horses, today
the Grandes Ecuries houses the Musée Vivant du Cheval
(the Living Horse Museum).

Inside, there are 31 rooms filled with paintings and
sculptures dedicated to horses and horsemanship. But
more than that, 30 horses and one donkey still live at the
stable. They're of varying breeds—Friesian, Appaloosa,
Spanish, Portuguese, Boulonnais, Thoroughbred, and even
Shetland ponies—and they perform a daily dressage
demonstration. They do tricks, too. Some of the museum's
horses can even sit and roll over.

The National Horse Racing Museum (England)

The large entrance gates at the National Horseracing Museum in Newmarket lead to a small building packed with exhibits. There are many paintings of famous English Thoroughbreds, but the museum also has some of the most unique (and macabre) exhibits in equine history:

- The preserved head of Persimmon, who won the Royal Derby in 1896.

- The skeleton of English racer Hyperion.

- The pistol Victorian jockey Fred Archer used to commit suicide.

- A model horse that visitors can saddle and bridle. (He never kicks or bites.)

- And, especially for Uncle John, the "seats for the loo" (toilet seats painted with horses and racing scenes), on sale in the museum gift shop.

Dartfield Horse Museum and Park (Ireland)

This museum is part of the 700-acre Dartfield estate, built in 1827. And despite the country's long equestrian history, this is the only museum dedicated to Ireland's horses. It features traditional exhibits, but Dartfield is also home to the country's largest population of Connemara ponies. Hardy and intelligent, the ponies are native to Galway and likely descendants of the Scandinavian ponies that the Vikings brought to Ireland in the eighth and ninth centuries.

The Equine Museum of Japan (Japan)

The ancient Japanese believed that the gods first appeared to humans on horseback. Since the fourth century, the Japanese have also ridden horses, and the Equine Museum on the island of Honshu celebrates that long history. The museum is located beside a park that was a racecourse during the mid-1800s—the first in Japan to feature European-style Thoroughbred horse racing.

The museum's exhibits are uniquely Japanese. There are ancient scrolls and statues that show horses participating in religious ceremonies, paintings of Kiso horses (Japan's favorite breed) in full battle armor, and the silver trophy that was the first Emperor's Cup of Japan. A special viewing device helps visitors understand how horses' vision differs from humans', and machines test human strength against the power of horses.

The International Museum of the Horse (Kentucky)

By far, though, the world's largest (52,000 square feet) and most comprehensive horse museum is in bluegrass country. Kentucky's International Museum of the Horse in Lexington includes exhibits on art and photography, a research library, Horseshoe Hall (a room adorned with hundreds of decorative and functional horseshoes), and a permanent collection that tells the story of the horse's evolution—from eohippus to the modern breeds.

Traveling exhibits stop by, too. Over the years, the

International Museum has hosted many temporary collections, including "Imperial China: Art of the Horse," worth more than $100 million and including a bronze chariot from the Han dynasty. "The Presidents and Their Horses" displayed quirky items like an electric horse that was once installed in President Calvin Coolidge's White House bedroom—he "rode" it dressed only in his underwear and a cowboy hat.

The museum is part of Kentucky Horse Park, a 1,200-acre horse farm where more than 40 different breeds are stabled. Standing at the park's entrance is a statue of Man o' War, who is buried on the property. Horses who live at the park's Hall of Champions—like Cigar, the greatest money winner in racing history—make appearances daily.

* * *

Hi-Yo, Scout . . . Away!

Everyone knows Silver, the Lone Ranger's horse, but what about Scout, the one Tonto rode?

- Scout was originally going to be solid white like Silver, but TV producers thought that made Silver less impressive. So they got a bay-and-white pinto to play Scout.

- In the early *Lone Ranger* radio programs, Tonto rode a horse named White Feller. But in a 1938 episode, the Lone Ranger (feeling bad for keeping Silver) released his horse into the wild. When Silver returned to his master, he brought along a friend for Tonto: Scout.

"Where the Turf Meets the Surf"

*Begun by Hollywood heavies wanting a vacation spot, the
Del Mar Racetrack today is a premier racing venue.*

Hollywood South

The 350-acre Del Mar racetrack, just north of San Diego,
California, is a horseshoe's throw from the Pacific Ocean, a
fact that inspired the track's slogan: "Where the Turf Meets
the Surf." It holds races from mid-July to early September
and typically hosts about 40,000 people per day.

The track got started in 1937, when movie-star crooner
Bing Crosby—along with fellow Tinseltown luminaries
like Pat O'Brien and Jimmy Durante and well-funded
friends like millionaire auto dealer Charles S. Howard—
founded the Del Mar Thoroughbred Club. At the time,
Crosby told reporters that he brought racing to Del Mar
because he and his pals were looking for a relaxed, sunny
place to spend their summers—away from the hectic pace
of Los Angeles.

The track opened that summer, and Crosby did more
than bask in the sun. On that first opening day, he stood
at the front gate to take tickets and greet visitors.

Track Cred

Del Mar might have been the brainchild of Hollywood celebrities, but it quickly gained a reputation as a serious racetrack. In August 1938, the track's second season, cofounder Charles Howard raced his Thoroughbred Seabiscuit at Del Mar in a much-publicized $25,000 winner-take-all race. In that contest, Seabiscuit battled it out with Ligaroti, a horse from Binglin Stables—a farm co-owned by Crosby and Lindsay Howard, Charles's son. Seabiscuit won the race by the proverbial nose and solidified Del Mar's reputation as one of the country's leading tracks.

It also gained a reputation for being a celebrity hangout. Stars like Lucille Ball, Desi Arnaz, W. C. Fields, Betty Grable, Ava Gardner, Bob Hope, and Dorothy Lamour made regular appearances at Del Mar in the 1940s and '50s. And today, Hollywood glitterati still take part in the Del Mar race scene—Leonardo DiCaprio, Brad Pitt, and Jessica Simpson have all been spotted there.

Notable Numbers

Over the years, Del Mar has posted some impressive stats:

• In 1949, Bill Shoemaker became the first apprentice jockey to win at Del Mar. (*More about him on page 208.*)

- In 1955, Cipria, a filly from Argentina, set a Del Mar record: she made $263.40 for each $2 bet.

- In 1991, the track hosted its most expensive race to date: the first $1 million Pacific Classic.

- On average, visitors to Del Mar place a total of more than $13 million in bets each day.

* * *

Taking the High Dive

Diving horses, who jumped from 30-foot-high platforms into a pool of water, got their start in the 1920s in Atlantic City, when sideshows made the act famous. By the 1950s, charges of animal cruelty made the shows unpopular; they shut down in the 1980s. But diving isn't completely foreign to horses—they sometimes do it in the wild. And there is one place where a horse can still take the plunge for show (and, by all accounts, be treated well): Magic Forest Amusement Park in Lake George, New York.

Lightning, a 13-year-old chestnut, lives at the park and, from June through August, performs two shows a day of about two minutes each. (He has the rest of the year off.) He inherited the job from his father, Red, who started diving at Magic Forest in 1977. According to the park, Lightning is trained to jump nine feet into a 14-foot-deep pool of water. And he's never prodded or pushed like the sideshow horses were (though his trainers do give him a bucket of oats after each plunge).

Unfinished Masterpiece

Created by Leonardo da Vinci, the Horse Statue would have been the largest equestrian monument on earth—if it had ever been built.

Leonardo's Great Idea

In the 1480s, Milan's Duke of Sforza commissioned Leonardo da Vinci to build a huge statue of a horse to honor his father, Francesco Sforza. Da Vinci worked on the piece for nearly 17 years, studying horses exhaustively and then making a series of models, including a full-sized clay model that was 24 feet tall. Next, he completed the molds, into which more than 50 tons of molten bronze would be poured to create the final horse. But then a war broke out, and metal was in short supply. All the bronze in Italy went to the war effort, mostly to make cannonballs.

On September 10, 1499, the French captured Milan, where da Vinci lived and worked at the time. Some soldiers camped near the artist's workshop, and a company of them used his clay horse model for target practice, riddling it with holes. Rainwater collected in the holes, and weather exposure eventually destroyed the model. When da Vinci died in 1519, he was "still mourning the loss of his great horse."

The Horse Rides . . . Finally

In 1977, an American named Charles Dent happened to pick up a copy of *National Geographic* magazine that contained an article on da Vinci and his horse. Dent, an Italian Renaissance buff, decided that completing the horse would be a fitting way to honor the greatest mind of the period.

Da Vinci had left no detailed drawings that indicated what the final horse was supposed to look like; all that survived were a diary and some preliminary sketches. No matter—Dent decided to wing it. On September 10, 1999, exactly 500 years after da Vinci was forced to abandon his dream, his horse (or at least an approximation) was unveiled in Milan. It stood 24 feet high, weighed 15 tons, and was made of bronze and stainless steel. The horse was intended, Dent explained, as a gift "to all the Italian people from the American people."

* * *

Horsey Hodge Podge

- In wild herds, the lead mare usually decides when the group should move to find food.
- Horses have about 175 bones in their bodies.
- Horses use more energy to lie down than to stand upright.
- On Hydra, in the Greek Isles, horses and ponies are the only legal means of transportation.

Mythconceptions: Pumpernickel

We went looking for the origins of this much-loved bread and discovered that two common myths surrounding its origins are deeply rooted in one very famous general . . . and his horse.

Myth #1: The bread name "pumpernickel" originated with Napoleon's horse.
Theory: During the Napoleonic wars of the early 1800s, French troops barely had enough bread to stave off famine. But there was always enough *pain* (bread) for Napoleon's horse Nicoll. Hence, *pain pour* (for) *Nicoll* . . . pumpernickel.

Myth #2: Napoleon again.
Theory: Another story goes that Napoleon didn't save the bread for his horse but that he thought the dense, coarse bread the soldiers had to eat on the battlefield wasn't fit for human consumption. Supposedly, on a military campaign in Eastern Europe, he discarded the bread, saying disdainfully that it was *"pain pour Nicoll"*—bread for Nicoll, his horse, meaning it was not good enough for humans to eat.

The truth: The term "pumpernickel" actually predates Napoleon by many years. The Germans were calling each other "pumpernickel" long before Napoleon was born. It was a derogatory term, similar to "jerk" in English. According to *Webster's Dictionary*, they began using the term for bread around 1756. It came from two old German words: *pumpern*, which means "to break wind," and *nickel*— "goblin" or "devil." Basically, people called it the "devil's fart" because the coarse, dark bread was so hard to digest.

*　*　*

Fact or Fiction?

The rumor: Adolf Hitler's chestnut stallion is buried at Louisiana's La Branche Plantation.

The evidence: There's no definitive proof that Nordlicht (North Light)—born in Germany in 1941—belonged to Hitler, but the circumstantial evidence is pretty good. Nordlicht was was named Germany's Horse of the Year in 1944 and even appeared on his own postage stamp. One of Hitler's supporters abandoned the horse when he fled Germany in 1945, and the Americans took Nordlicht to the States with them. Louisiana doctor and horse breeder C. Walter Mattingly bought the horse in 1948 and moved him to La Branche. When Nordlicht died in 1968, he was buried at the plantation. Today, the owners of La Branche proudly profess the "grave of Hitler's horse" as one of the plantation's attractions.

Equine Expressions

At one time, horses were an integral part of human culture. So it's no wonder that they show up in all kinds of phrases. Here are some favorites.

Hold Your Horses

Meaning: Be patient, take your time.

Origin: This is a born-and-bred American expression. The phrase first appeared in print in an 1844 edition of a Louisiana newspaper: "Hold your hosses, Squire. There's no use gettin' riled, no how." ("Hoss" was 19th-century slang for horse.) By the 1930s, the phrase we know today—"hold your horses"—was showing up in common speech.

A Stalking Horse

Meaning: A decoy, specifically a political candidate used to conceal another person's real candidacy.

Origin: In 16th-century England, hunters discovered that it was easier to find game if they hid behind a horse than if they went off into the woods by themselves—birds and other animals would run from humans, but not horses. So hunters stood behind the neck or crouched under the belly of a horse trained to graze as it slowly approached wild game. That way, the hunter could get a good shot before the game noticed him.

Take the Bit Between Your Teeth

Meaning: Take control.

Origin: Bits press against the soft part of a horse's mouth as the rider manipulates the reins, directing the animal which way to go. But a horse who takes a bit between his teeth chomps down on the fitting and takes control away from the rider. This phrase first appeared in John Dryden's 1682 poem "The Medal":

> But this new Jehu spurs the hot-mounted horse,
> Instructs the beast to know his native force,
> To take the bit between his teeth and fly
> To the next headlong steep of anarchy.

It originally meant to convey obstinance. But over the years, it evolved to a more positive expression of taking charge.

Long in the Tooth

Meaning: Old

Origin: Back in the 19th century, horse traders were a shifty bunch who often tried to pass off old horses as younger than they were. The best way for a buyer to identify a horse's true age was to inspect the animal's teeth to see how long and yellow they were and how far the gums had receded.

189

If the roots of the teeth were showing, the buyer knew the horse was old.

Examining horses' teeth gave us two other expressions:

- **"Straight from the horse's mouth."** Because young horses were worth more than old ones, looking in the animal's mouth was a reliable way to establish its value.
- **"Don't look a gift horse in the mouth."** When you got a horse as a gift, checking its teeth right there in front of the gift-giver was bad manners.

You Can Lead a Horse to Water, but You Can't Make Him Drink

Meaning: You can show someone the best path, but you can't force him to take it.

Origin: This expression dates back to 1546, when an early version appeared in John Heywood's *A Dialogue Conteinyng the Number in Effect of All the Prouerbes in the Englishe Tongue*: "A man maie well bring a horse to the water. But he cannot make him drinke without he will."

*   *   *

Quite a Storm

Born in 1983, the Thoroughbred stallion Storm Cat entered stud in 1988. His initial fee: $30,000. His children and grandchildren, though, proved to be such great racers (160 stakes winners) that by the time he retired in 2008, he was making a record $500,000 for each mating.

Good Grooms

Grooms are perhaps the hardest-working laborers at the racetrack. They are the trainers and jockeys' eyes and ears and the horses' best friends. But they're also among the industry's least-appreciated professionals.

Unsung Heroes

In the racetrack pecking order, grooms generally rank just above stable hands and exercise boys and are rarely rewarded for the relationships they develop with their horses. A few lucky grooms might get a percentage of a horse's winnings—maybe 1 percent—in addition to their wages (usually between $400 and $600 per week), but that's the exception. Long hours, huge responsibilities, modest wages, and no job security are the norm.

Some grooms have just one equine charge (usually a high-profile racehorse), but most are responsible for six to eight horses. Their daily chores include preparing feed, monitoring diet, and tending to aches, pains, bruises, and strains. They check a horse's shoes and tack for wear, prepare the animal for exercise and races, and advise the trainer and jockey. Because the horse's health and performance are paramount, everyone depends greatly on the groom's close attention.

Shorty and Secretariat

Triple Crown winner Secretariat and his groom Eddie "Shorty" Sweat were buddies. Secretariat was not a "people" horse. He was high-strung, demanding, and intelligent, and often nipped passersby. Sweat calmed his nerves, soothing his anxieties with quiet conversation. He even sometimes slept on a cot outside the racing champion's stall.

Every morning, horse and groom greeted each other with a shake—Sweat's hand and Secretariat's outstretched tongue. The two times that Secretariat finished out of first place, the horse stood facing the back of his stall until Sweat came by to bolster his spirits. And whenever Secretariat flew cross-country for races, Sweat was responsible for loading him onto the plane and accompanying him on the journey . . . at his side the whole time.

Sweat also shared a little of Secretariat's spotlight. After the 1973 Kentucky Derby, Sweat got to come out from

behind the backstretch to walk Secretariat into the winner's circle. And when a life-size bronze statue of Secretariat was unveiled at the Kentucky Horse

Park, it included jockey Ron Turcotte aboard and Eddie Sweat leading the horse.

Not for the Weak

Susan Esseltine, from Ontario's Western Fair Raceway, won the title of Groom of the Year in 2006. A well-known figure around the paddock, she's spent 30 years at the track. Her father ran Western Fair's tack shop, and at 15, Esseltine started mucking stalls. She became a groom soon after.

Esseltine usually works at least 12 hours a day. She begins at dawn, and if one of her horses runs on a night racing card, she may not have the horse paddocked before 1:00 a.m. Esseltine is particularly remarkable, though, because she's also fighting leukemia. Each week she takes a day off to obtain treatment at the local cancer clinic, yet as the next day dawns, she's back at the track—business as usual. Esseltine may not make lots of money at her job, but she and other grooms sign up for the other benefit: the relationships they develop with the horses in their care.

*   *   *

Go Greek

The ancient Greeks were avid horsepeople who introduced four-horse chariot races to the Olympics in 680 BC. Men started competing in the Olympics on horseback around the same time.

A Nice Day for a Ride

*Since the mid-1930s, visitors to New York City have been able to
take carriage horse rides through Central Park. At only $34
for a half-hour, it may seem like a steal. But some say
that for the horses, it's no walk in the park.*

A holdover from the Victorian era, when horses were
used as a primary means of transportation, carriage
horse rides have long been associated with the romance
and mystique of New York City. It's difficult to say exactly
when the tradition began—records indicate it was in full
swing by 1935, though drivers likely offered rides even
before that—but since then, it's become a staple of city
life. It's also created a lot of controversy.

Park and Ride

As of 2006 (the last count taken), 221 horses were
licensed to give rides in Central Park. The city also
licenses the drivers (293 of them) and the carriages they
pull (68, ranging from Cinderella–style to hansom cabs).

The city keeps the horses' activities fairly well regu-
lated, too, at least on paper. The laws surrounding carriage
horses are as follows:

- Horses can work no more than nine hours a day and
  must get a 15-minute rest period every two hours.

- No horses are allowed to work when the temperature is below 19°F or above 89°F. In the winter, blankets must be put over horses when they aren't giving rides. In adverse weather, horses must be sent back to the stables (although the definition of "adverse" is open to interpretation).

- Horses who are lame or ill cannot work.

- Carriage horse rides are prohibited between 7:00 a.m. and 10:00 a.m. Monday through Friday to avoid any conflicts with rush-hour traffic. From 10:00 a.m. to 9:00 p.m. Monday through Friday, carriage horses are allowed only in Central Park and nowhere else in the city.

- Horses are never allowed on bridges or inside tunnels.

The Problem

Sounds good, right? Well, the ASPCA and other animal-rights groups don't think so. In June 2007, New York City comptroller William C. Thompson Jr. released an 18-page audit of the city's carriage horse industry and found some problems. Some drivers ignored many of the laws. (After all, no one except the carriage driver can ensure that the horses get their breaks.) The average working life of a carriage horse was four years (as compared to the 15-year working life of horses in the city's mounted police force). Many horses weren't given enough water, illness and injuries were often overlooked, veterinary care was sometimes absent, and paperwork certifying the horses wasn't always properly maintained.

The Other Side

The report led to a wave of criticism, and several groups (including the ASPCA) called for a ban of carriage horses altogether. Carriage horses have already been banned in Paris, London, Beijing, and other major cities—either to prevent accidents, to avoid traffic congestion, or because of complaints about mistreatment of the animals. The ASPCA wanted New York to follow suit.

But the Horse and Carriage Association of New York, a group that represents the owners of carriage horses in the city, said that the industry treats its horses well and works hard to ensure that animals are healthy—in fact, after working in the carriage industry, the horses are usually retired to farms. And in March 2008, the group hired a veterinarian to check on horses at five stables in the city. He said that all the horses were healthy and well cared for.

And so the debate over horse-drawn carriages continues, but the practice remains popular in New York. For his part, Thompson, who initiated the audit, called for a balance between the two sides: "The carriage-horse industry is an important part of our City's charm and appeal for New Yorkers and tourists alike. The City must take its role more seriously to ensure the health and well-being of carriage-horses and the regulation of the industry in general."

*　　*　　*

Mares can give birth in as few as 15 minutes.

The Mongol Express

*During the 13th century, the Mongols kept track
of their empire from the backs of horses.*

The Yam

Horses were central to the Mongols' culture and economic
well-being. Geldings were used for riding; mares for food
and as draft animals. Mare's milk was a staple in their diet.
And by becoming the Middle Ages' most expert horsemen,
the Mongols managed to control a vast area that stretched
from the Yellow Sea to the Mediterranean. Beginning with
the conquests of Genghis Khan around 1200, their territory
ultimately encompassed more than 12 million square miles.

The Mongols built that empire using a combination of
armed conquest and negotiated trade deals—the latter
often agreed to under threat of the former. Both techniques
required fast, efficient communication between the central
government, namely the khan (or ruler), and his armies
and emissaries. So the Mongols developed the *yam* system,
in which couriers on horseback carried messages from relay
station to relay station, in much the same way the
American Pony Express did centuries later.

Easier Said Than Done

Simple as the concept was, carrying it out wasn't easy. The

khan established relay stations every 25 miles. Each station maintained a stock of 400 fresh horses for the couriers, who traded horses to make sure that the animals were always rested enough to perform at peak speeds.

The horses were bedraggled, sinewy, clumsy-looking runts, almost small enough to be considered ponies by modern Western standards. But their toughness and stamina more than made up for their lack of good looks and size. They could survive climates from subarctic to equatorial and managed nicely in rugged mountains or desolate deserts. They weren't picky eaters either, and remained independent enough to forage on their own.

Only the Best

Riders selected as yam couriers were the empire's best horsemen: strong, young, and skilled. They had to be. Some trips required only 50 to 70 miles a day, but distances of 200 to 250 miles were not uncommon. One rider carried his message the full, grueling distance. The riders were even strapped into their saddles to make sure they stayed on task.

At the height of the Mongol Empire, the yam network covered more than 187,000 miles and employed as many as 3 million horses. It lasted throughout the period of the Mongols' rule and remained intact, though cut back, until the empire crumbled in the 15th century.

Saddle Up!

*The Chinese were harnessing and riding horses as early as
4000 BC, but they rode bareback. The first saddles—
a strip of animal hide or a piece of heavy cloth—
weren't developed until much later.*

Not So Easy Riders

Arguments rage over who invented the first saddles—some
say it was the nomadic Scythians from Siberia, others
claim it was the ancient Greeks, and the Moors in North
Africa often get credit. But the Assyrians (from modern-
day Syria, Iran, Iraq, and Turkey) were certainly among
the first. Around 700 BC, Assyrian warriors went into
battle riding on thick, decorative riding pads, and they
used straps that resembled modern girths. The Mongols
followed with a primitive saddle tree and a padded felt
saddle on a wooden frame.

A saddle that included four horns, complete with a
solid saddle tree, emerged from the Roman Empire around
AD 200. But the first saddle that's most like the ones we
know today belonged to the Sarmatians, a nomadic Indo-
Iranian people from central Asia. Around AD 365, the
Sarmatians appeared with a saddle that included a saddle
tree, breastplate, girth, and metal stirrups.

European Invasion

It was the Mongols who brought the Sarmatian saddle to Europe. In the fourth century, Mongol Huns battled the Sarmatians in Asia, adopted their saddle design, and introduced it to new cultures when they invaded southeastern Europe. Over the next few centuries, Europeans used the Sarmatian saddle in battle, tournaments, and even during the Crusades. It wasn't until chivalrous medieval knights needed to excel on horseback while dressed in full armor and carrying an arsenal of weapons that the saddle changed again.

The result was a wooden tree with a higher pommel and cantle that kept the knight securely seated and balanced on his horse during battle. For comfort, the saddles were padded with wool or horsehair and covered with leather, untanned hides, or sturdy fabrics. Elaborate leatherwork, precious metals, jewels, tokens, and embroidery denoted a knight's rank, and metal stirrups helped him keep control of his horse.

Are You Western or English?

The saddle remained largely unchanged for several centuries. But by the 1800s, its evolution had divided. The primary reason for the split: the saddle horn. Cowboys needed a horn at the front of the saddle to secure their lassos, and the military used it for leverage and balance while they were fighting on horseback. With one hand firmly gripped on the saddle horn, the soldiers could fight enemies and not fall off their horses. So in the 19th century, these groups developed the Western saddle, which had a horn and two strong cinches holding the saddle firmly on the horse. Western saddles were heavier than English saddles and covered more of the horses' back.

The English saddle has no horn. Its padding (leather cowhide or pigskin) is built over layers of wood usually reinforced with spring steel. English saddles are smaller, lighter, and designed to give the rider close contact with the horse.

Giddyap!

Today, saddles come in many styles—dressage, jumping, roping, show saddles—and in sizes to fit any rider and breed of horse. But deciding which saddle to use is a very personal choice. For most equestrians, borrowing a saddle is like borrowing someone else's shoes—it might work in a pinch, but it'll never really fit.

* * *

Horse of a Different Color

You can't predict a horse's adult color when it's a foal. All horses change color several times when they're young, finally settling on a shade when they're about two years old.

More Military Mounts

Here are two more military horse heroes

Last Horse Standing . . . Sort Of

During the Indian Wars of the 19th century, Myles Keogh, a captain in the U.S. 7th Cavalry, rode a mustang/Morgan horse named Comanche. The horse was fast, strong, and brave, and Keogh gave him his name after a particularly fierce fight with a Comanche tribe in Kansas. The horse was wounded in the battle, but he let Keogh keep riding— and fighting.

In 1876, Keogh and his men took off for the Battle of the Little Bighorn (Custer's Last Stand). Keogh rode Comanche, of course, but the battle was a disaster for the cavalry. The Cheyenne and Lakota tribes soundly defeated them, and Custer (who led the charge) was killed. Keogh also died, but two days after the fight was over, Comanche emerged, severely wounded but alive.

Nursing him back to health took months, but the horse eventually recovered. The U.S. military then officially retired him to a life of luxury—during his retirement he was fed a regular diet of "whisky bran mash and buckets of beer." Comanche died in 1897 at the age of 29. His loyalty and stoicism led to stories that he was the only military survivor at Little Bighorn, but he wasn't. Apparently, several of the other horses and a bulldog also survived the battle. Comanche remains the most famous, though, and the most revered: he was the first of two horses in U.S. history to be buried with full military honors.

The Sentimental Favorite

The second horse buried with full honors? Black Jack. If any military horse can be said to have captured American hearts in the 20th century, it was Black Jack. Named after General John "Black Jack" Pershing of World War I fame, the Morgan/quarter horse was born in 1947 and was the last horse to carry the "U.S." brand of the army.

Black Jack was the riderless horse who attended the funerals of four presidents (Herbert Hoover, John F. Kennedy, Dwight Eisenhower, and Lyndon Johnson) and one general (Douglas MacArthur). It was Kennedy's funeral procession, though, that made Black Jack famous. Millions of people worldwide watched him following behind the president's casket, the boots and stirrups he carried turned backward. Black Jack retired from military service in 1973 and died in 1976.

For more military horses,
turn to page 155.

*   *   *

Wild horse herds usually have just one stallion.

Life in the Pits

*For more than 100 years, ponies worked for their supper
in the coal mines of Britain and North America.*

A Dirty Job

In March 2007, an historic obituary crossed the desks of
British newspapers. Sparky—36 years old, the last of
Britain's deep-pit coal ponies—had died.

Sparky began at the mines when he was four years old
and was a pit pony for 13 years. During his working years,
he hauled ore carts—sometimes four at a time. He also
hauled mine timbers and heavy machinery. Sparky sometimes had to work without light, and he often wore a steel
helmet because part of his job was bumping open ventila-
tion doors as he made his way along the narrow shafts.

Sparky was a typical deep-pit pony. At shift's end, he
retired to underground stables that many miners said were
nicer than their own accommodations. The animals ate
high-quality food and always had access to fresh water.
The ponies did live underground for years and some never
saw the sun, but many mine bosses so valued the animals
that miners who mistreated them were fired immediately—even if the ponies were so bold as to steal a miner's
lunch (which they often did).

Small Stature, Big Heart

Before coal mines in Britain and North America became mechanized in the mid-20th century, pit ponies were indispensable to the industry. The little horses could get into places men couldn't and hauled cartfuls of ore from the drifts to the mine head.

The animals varied in size from Shetlands to Fells, depending on the height and width of the mine shafts. They were bred particularly for strength and a calm disposition. Long necks helped too, especially in sections where ceilings were low and the ponies had to duck to pass.

Laws required that pit ponies be four years old when they went to work in the mines, but most were at least five—mine owners wanted them to be strong and fully mature. The animals came from a variety of places: The English imported Shetlands from Scotland. The

Americans brought in ponies from Finland, and in Canada's maritime provinces, most of the ponies were bred locally. Not all made the grade, however. The most sturdy, tireless, docile, and easily trained were the most desirable picks because work areas were tight, and an aggressive or temperamental pony could endanger miners and the other animals.

Who's the Boss?

That doesn't mean the ponies didn't have personality. One pony in England's Durham coalfields never gave his usual driver a problem, but when a new driver was assigned to him, the pony misbehaved. At every sharp turn on a narrow underground rail line, the pony sped up, tipping the coal carts. That stopped all traffic in the pony's section of the mine. And while the driver set the carts back on the tracks and re-loaded the ore, the pony waited patiently . . . periodically glancing over his shoulder to see how his cursing driver was progressing.

Another pony, accustomed to pulling three carts at a time, permitted his driver to hook up a fourth for the last run before the end of the shift at their mine in Alberta, Canada. One day, the driver slyly hooked up a fifth. As the pony started out, the first cart moved on the rails and then came the second, third, and fourth. But when the pony felt the fifth, he stopped immediately and wouldn't budge. His wise driver unhooked the fifth cart and, as a gesture of appeasement, also the fourth. As soon as he did, the pony went back to work.

Danger! Danger!

Life in the pits could be dangerous. All the hazards miners faced (roof collapses, floods, and so on) could also harm the animals. A Canadian miner named Joe Guidolin remembered saving a group of ponies during a 1948 flood. The snow aboveground had melted and seeped into the mine. By the time Guidolin got to the pony stable, the water was up to the animals' bellies. He organized the ponies into a single-file line, tied the tail of one to the bridle of another, and urged them on to safety. He said, "I knew for sure that they were afraid. I wished that I could have explained it all to them, but even still, they trusted me enough to follow me out." All 16 of the mine's ponies survived.

End of an Era

In the 1950s, as increased mechanization became essential to stay competitive, mines started phasing out the ponies. In the United States, the last coal pony emerged from Iowa's New Gladstone Mine in 1971. Progress was slower in Britain and Canada. There, the last ponies didn't leave until the early 1990s.

Life after the mines was usually good for the ponies. Because they were so well trained, they were in high demand as riding and carriage ponies. And most, like Sparky, enjoyed many years of relative leisure after they retired.

The Shoe

*The oldest man to win the Kentucky Derby, Bill Shoemaker
was also one of the smallest. Check out the life and
times of America's most famous jockey.*

During his 41-year career, jockey Bill "the Shoe"
Shoemaker won five Belmont Stakes, four
Kentucky Derbys, and two Preakness Stakes. He rode in
more than 40,000 races and won 8,833 of them, a record
that stood until 1999 when Laffit Pincay Jr. broke it. In
all, Shoemaker won more than $120 million in purses
and had a reputation for being gifted with horses—his
firm but gentle hand was just what the animals needed to
be coaxed first over the finish line again and again.

Smaller Than a Breadbox

Shoemaker was born in Texas in 1931. He weighed only 1
pound, 13 ounces, at birth and no one expected him to
make it to the next morning. (One legend says that his
grandmother put in him a box on the stove to keep him
warm.) He survived, though, and grew into a healthy but
small child. After his parents divorced, Shoemaker moved
with his father to California, and it was there that he fell in
love with horses.

As a teenager, Shoemaker got a job as a stable and exercise boy and then quickly moved up to jockey. He was a perfect size: under 100 pounds and just 4'11". His first professional race was in March 1949, and his first win came a month later. Of that race, Shoemaker said, "I almost went into shock. She was a chestnut filly, and you bet I remember her. I think I got about 10 dollars."

Derby Darling

Shoemaker's first Kentucky Derby win came in 1955 on a chestnut stallion named Swaps. But it was his 1957 Derby loss that got most people talking. That year, Shoemaker mistook a furlong post for the finish and slowed his horse (Gallant Man) just a few feet too soon. He lost when Iron Liege raced up from behind and beat them by a nose. It was an embarrassment for sure, but also a mistake other jockeys understood. Said Eddie Arcaro, "After the race, they did what they should have done 50 years before. They put lines on the fence to show the finish." And five weeks later, Shoemaker and Gallant Man won the Belmont by eight lengths.

Shoemaker won the Derby again in 1959 and 1965, but then seemed to slow down. He broke his leg in 1968 when a horse threw him, and a year later, he was injured again when a horse trampled him in the paddock. During the 1970s, Shoemaker seemed fated for retirement. But then, in 1986, along came a horse named Ferdinand.

Ferdinand was a long shot (17–1 odds at the 1986

209

Kentucky Derby), but Shoemaker thought they had a chance. Maybe it was his skill with horses that gave him that confidence. According to Jay Hovdey, one of Shoemaker's friends,

> There's a lot for the horse to be worried about [during a race] . . . What Shoemaker did, he had an innate light touch, a very sensitive touch with his hands. The hands were on the reins, the reins were on the bit, and the bit was in the horse's mouth. That's the way Shoemaker communicated in a very gentle, very insinuating kind of command that the horse needed and responded to.

It worked. Ferdinand lagged behind out of the starting gate, but going into the backstretch, he started to advance. Shoemaker urged the horse on and, at the top of the stretch, found a hole. They navigated through traffic and took the lead . . . eventually winning by 2½ lengths. It was a victory that capped Shoemaker's already remarkable career. He was 54, the oldest jockey to win the Derby. (Tragically, Ferdinand's later life became a catalyst for the racehorse-rescue movement. For more on that story, turn to page 123.)

Out to Pasture

Shoemaker retired from racing in 1990 and began training horses. Ultimately, he trained 157 winners. He died in 2003, but his legacy as a racing hero was firmly established. He was also humble. Of his skills on the racetrack, Shoemaker once said, "I never felt I was gifted. I got the right horses at the right time, and that made me good."

Hold Your Horses

Who would have thought those plastic horse toys you played with as a kid would become collectibles and even inspire their own counterculture?

Hey! That's Not a Toy!

Breyer horses started out as decorations, not toys. In 1950, a Chicago-based manufacturer called the Breyer Molding Company began making plastic horses and animals to decorate clocks and lamps. Its first model—the #57 Western Horse—went to the F. W. Woolworth Company as part of a mantel clock. But soon, the company was flooded with letters about children removing the horse models to play with them and parents wondering where they could buy just the horses. By the late 1950s, the company had changed its name (to Breyer Animal Creations) and was making toys instead of decorations. Since then, Breyer has produced hundreds of molds, representing thousands of different horse breeds and colors.

Each Breyer horse begins its life as a hand-sculpted clay model that is then transformed into a steel mold. Workers inject hot, sturdy plastic into the mold, and when it cools, the basic horse body is ready. In the old days, artists hand-painted the models—from the eyes to the hooves—but today, workers use stencils to airbrush on the horses' features. By the time a Breyer horse arrives in a child's hands, about 20 different artisans have played a part in its creation.

Breyer makes nearly 5 million plastic horses every year. And the company has branched out into porcelain horses, plush horses, tack, and other barnyard animals.

Where's the Auction?

Of course, a product that's so unique and of such high quality attracts more than just children. Collectors of all ages flock to stores to buy up new Breyer horses. These sell for anywhere from $5 to more than $100. But it's the old models that people really want.

Vintage Breyers are fairly easy to find . . . thanks to online auctions, antique malls, swap meets, and flea markets. And Web sites like eBay are a plastic equine goldmine, where the horses sometimes go for as much as $2,000.

There's the (Paint) Rub

The condition and age of a model can determine its value. According to collector Melissa Gilkey Mince, "If the horse is a common one, paint rubs are the death-knell of value. Rubs are tolerated in extremely rare models; however, the value plummets sharply because collectors will always be looking for an 'upgrade' and want to be sure they can sell the damaged horse for the same price they paid."

Another way to find out a model's age is to check its hind legs. Breyers made after 1960 have a company logo stamped on their inner hind leg. These marks have changed at least 20 times over the years, and based on the logo's design, collectors can tell when a model was first sold. (It's also a good way to pick out fakes.)

Magazines and Merriment

Of course, all these collectors need a place to swap stories. So every two months, Breyer puts out a magazine called *Just About Horses*, dedicated to its model horses. The magazine includes stats on upcoming molds, color schemes for vintage models, articles about collecting, and a "blast to the past" feature about a select model each issue.

When the collectors are finished reading, they head out to their very own convention: BreyerFest. For one weekend in late July, thousands of Breyer fanatics converge on the Kentucky Horse Park in Lexington for a company-hosted gathering. During BreyerFest, collectors can meet the artists behind the equines, watch live horse shows, and see the real horses who inspire Breyer molds. For many Breyer collectors, this is one event neither they nor their model horses—there are also shows and swaps—like to miss.

*   *   *

The horse is New Jersey's state animal.

The Thunder Down Under

Australia's Melbourne Cup is considered to be the most prestigious two-mile handicap race in the world and the second-richest turf race. It's also "the race that stops a nation," making Melbourne the only city that has a public holiday for a horse race.

History: In the 1861 inaugural race, 17 horses competed for approximately £170 ($325) cash . . . and a gold watch.

Racetrack: Flemington Racecourse, Melbourne, Australia

Date: First Tuesday in November. It was officially made a public holiday in 1877.

Course: 3,200 meters (1.988 miles) as of 1972. Originally the track was more than two miles long, but that changed when Australia adopted the metric system.

Field: Three-year-olds and up; as many as 24 horses

Purse: Approximately $4.87 million (U.S.), sponsored through 2010 by Emirates Airlines (with a bonus of $467,000 if the winner can also win Ireland's St. Leger race in same year). The trophy awarded since 1919 is a three-handled gold cup worth about $80,000. Made of 34 pieces of metal, it contains 3.6 pounds of 18-carat gold hand-beaten for more than 200 hours.

Notable Jockeys

- The first Aboriginal jockey to win the race was J. Cutts, who took the title at the first and second Melbourne Cups riding Archer in 1861 and 1862.
- The second Aboriginal jockey to win was 13-year-old Peter St. Albans, riding Briseis in 1876.
- Most wins by a jockey: Bobby Lewis and Harry White are tied with four each.

Traditions

- About 80 percent of Australia's population wagers on the race. Sweepstakes are held throughout the country, with ticketholders randomly matched with horses for a chance to win a prize. Thus, almost everyone has a stake in the race.
- "Fashions on the Field" is a major focus of racing day, with prizes awarded for the best-dressed male and female racegoers. In 1965, the miniskirt received worldwide publicity when model Jean Shrimpton wore one on Derby Day during Melbourne Cup week.

Milestones

1876: The three-year-old filly Briseis set a record that still stands: she won three prestigious Australian races—the Victorian Derby, the Melbourne Cup, and the VRC Oaks (now the Crown Oaks) in the span of six days.

1910: Comedy King became the first foreign-bred horse to win the cup.

1990: The present record holder is Kingston Rule, with a time of 3 minutes, 6.3 seconds.

2003: A record attendance of 122,736 racegoers.

2005: Makybe Diva became the only horse to win the race three times—from 2003 to 2005.

Did You Know?

- The first cup winner, Archer, was rumored to have walked 500 miles from Nowra, New South Wales, to Melbourne in order to compete. An Australian movie about him called *Archer's Adventure* features an 18-year-old Nicole Kidman.

- Phar Lap (beloved in Australia, but actually from New Zealand), the most famous horse in the world of his day, won the 1930 Melbourne Cup. He also competed in 1929 and 1931, when he came in third and eighth, respectively. Phar Lap died in 1932, supposedly poisoned by gangsters.

- A new trophy is created each year and becomes the property of the winning owner. (A second cup is on hand in the event of a tie.)

- Flemington Racecourse grows more than 12,000 rose-bushes in 200 varieties within its large expanse. Each major race day at Flemington has an official flower—for the Melbourne Cup, it's the yellow rose.

A Horse, Of Course

Five facts about the famous Mr. Ed.

1. The golden palomino's real name was Bamboo Harvester, and he was born in California in 1949.

2. Every day, Mr. Ed ate 20 pounds of hay and drank a gallon of sweet tea.

3. The horse didn't obey anyone except his trainer, Les Hilton, so Hilton had to be on the set at all times, telling Ed where to look, how to move, and what do to. On the show (which ran from 1961 to 1966), even when it seems like Ed is involved in what's going on, he's really just looking at Hilton off-screen.

4. Ed did most of his own stunts. He was trained to do everything from opening the barn door to answering the telephone.

5. The horse couldn't talk, however. His trainer used a nylon bit to get him to move his lips. (The rumor that Hilton gave the horse peanut butter to make him lick his lips isn't true.)

Good Breeding

How well are you clued in to horse breeds? Four of them are waiting to be revealed in this crossword. Give yourself free rein to solve.
(Answers on page 226.)

ACROSS

1. Bogus
5. La ___ (Milan opera house)
10. Groups for soccer moms et al.
14. It springs eternal
15. Like every crossword answer
16. Troop group
17. Scalawags
18. German breed often seen in the Olympics
20. Slangy good-bye
22. ___ pentameter
23. Nigeria's capital
24. Fireplace guards
25. String in a string quartet
27. Gas and oil, e.g.
28. Figure skater Midori
29. Layout
31. Like maple trees
35. Skip a turn
37. "Air Music" composer Ned ___

39. Classic soft drink
40. Easily split rock
42. Matadors' foes
44. Shoot the breeze
45. More peculiar
47. Flinches, e.g.
49. Window over a door
52. Baker's dozen?
53. Soprano Farrell
54. They gambol a lot
57. Old Spanish breed, the mount of kings
59. Song in an opera house
60. A thou
61. Uptight
62. "Who killed ___ Robin?"
63. Steak order
64. Guru followers
65. Leg joint

DOWN

1. The Flying Dutchman, e.g.
2. Last word in *The Wizard of Oz*
3. Nez Perce horse

4. Peyote source
5. Big beer glass
6. Santa follower
7. Mother's sister, to her niece
8. Sign of summer
9. Consultant's offering
10. It's good on pasta
11. *Survivor* group
12. At full speed
13. Lip-___ (fake singing)
19. Some peers
21. Shield: Var.
24. Excellent
25. CEOs and such
26. Slanted: Abbr.
27. Uproar
30. Carved pole

32. French draft horse
33. It's cool
34. Chihuahua sounds
36. Alley Oop's time
38. Glacial drifts
41. Detroit dud
43. Sinks below the horizon
46. Dunkable treats
48. Antiaircraft fire
49. "Coffee, ___ me?"
50. Actress Lisa (*Melrose Place*)
51. Tree of the birch family
52. Cheeky
54. Stool pigeon
55. Paddy crop
56. Japanese rice wine
58. Number after cinque

Tackle This!

We bet you know the difference between a crupper and a snaffle. But can you find those bits of tack and 26 others in the puzzle?

BIT	LIP STRAP
BLINDERS	MARTINGALE
BRIDLE	NOSEBAND
CANTLE	POMMEL
CAPARISON	REINS
CHAMBON	SADDLE
CROP	SALLONG
CROWNPIECE	SHANK HOBBLE
CRUPPER	SNAFFLE
D RING	SPURS
GIRTH	STIRRUP
HACKAMORE	SURCINGLE
HALTER	TRACES
HARNESS	TREE

```
            I
            K
            L P       M
        E B F       E G
      H S K E D L E
    A C S L V S T L A
    Y H Z D P P Q N F G
    M T I Y S A C A F I R
  N B R E P P U R C A C P
Y M B I M Y U M O T N Q U F
R A L Z G X F R A W J S Q R D N
O X E L D D A S R N C D P R Q R B
P K M I T Q Q   T P R S N I E R H
P S M D T O     I I O D D T L L A
  R O Q D       N E P N L S G N C J
  I P           G G C U A S S N O K Y
            B L X A E H B P E I B A Q
          G N O L L A S E G N C M M H
        B L I N D E R S S Z R R A O U
      I G C A P A R I S O N A U H R A
    T R E E L B B O H K N A H S C E T
```

For answers, turn to page 226.

Answers

The Horse Lingo IQ Test, page 34

1. Spook
2. Ten
3. Calves
4. Feet
5. Won his first race
6. Black
7. The mare. Only female horses run in distaff races.
8. His weight
9. They buck.
10. His mane has been clipped short.

Track Duty, page 108

1. b
2. a
3. c
4. a
5. b
6. c

Singing Their Praises, page 132

1. America, "A Horse with No Name." When this song came out in 1972, some radio stations wouldn't play it because "horse" is a slang term for "heroin." (The band assured the media and public that the song was indeed about a horse.)

2. Michael Martin Murphey, "Wildfire." Besides writing this #1 hit, Murphey also composed "The Land of Enchantment," New Mexico's state ballad.

3. Kenny Loggins, "All the Pretty Little Ponies." This children's song was first released on the 1994 album *Return to Pooh Corner*, which also included tunes by John Lennon and Phil Collins.

4. The Byrds, "The Chestnut Mare." Founding band member Roger McGuinn (formerly Jim McGuinn) changed his name after joining the Subud religious group in the mid-1960s. (The group's leader thought he needed a new name.) The change confused some of McGuinn's fans, who thought "Roger" must have been "Jim's" brother.

5. John Denver, "Eagles and Horses." John Denver was extremely interested in space travel—he even took and passed NASA's physical exam, in the hopes of becoming the first civilian in space, but he died in 1997 before he could make the trip.

6. Johnny Cash, "Tennessee Stud." Although the "Man in Black" had a reputation suggesting otherwise, he spent only one night in jail—for bringing methamphetamines into the United States from Mexico.

7. Garth Brooks, "Wild Horses." Country maverick Garth Brooks attended Oklahoma State University on a partial athletic scholarship as a javelin thrower. The lure of singing in clubs was too much during college, however, and he gave up sports to concentrate on music.

8. Don Fogelberg, "Run for the Roses." Fogelberg's father was a high school band teacher, and although Fogelberg eventually came to be thankful for his early musical training, he used to fake sports injuries to get out of piano practice.

Horse Sense, page 175

1. Black Beauty—Anna Sewell felt that her audience for *Black Beauty* would be people who worked with horses. She wanted to alert them to the industry's inhumane practices (the use of whips, checkreins, and other devices) and once said that she wrote the book to "induce kindness, sympathy, and an understanding treatment of horses." Children, how-ever, loved the story, and quickly after its publication, *Black Beauty* became a children's classic.

2. Flicka—In the 1943 film *My Friend Flicka*, Roddy McDowall stars as young, dreamy Ken McLaughlin, who picks the wild, part-mustang Flicka for his own. McDowall starred in another animal-friendly film (1943's *Lassie Come Home*), which costarred another animal-loving child actor: Elizabeth Taylor. (See #5.)

3. Trigger—His original name was Golden Cloud, but Roy Rogers renamed him because the palomino was quick-footed and quick-witted.

4. Buttermilk—This horse died in 1972 (at the age of 31) but was stuffed, mounted, and put on display at the Roy Rogers and Dale Evans Museum in Branson, Missouri.

5. The Pie—Elizabeth Taylor was just 11 years old when she filmed *National Velvet*, her first starring role.

6. Seabiscuit—Seabiscuit got his name from his father, the feisty Thoroughbred Hard Tack. A "seabiscuit" is another name for hardtack, a crackerlike biscuit that sailors ate on long sea voyages.

7. Sophie—Many different horse actors played Sophie on M*A*S*H, and even though she's a mare on the show, she was usually played by a male horse.

8. Misty—Misty's foal Stormy, who was born in 1962, got his name from the Ash Wednesday Storm, a violent Nor'easter that struck Chincoteague Island just before Misty gave birth.

9. The Black Stallion—Between 1945 and 1989, Walter Farley wrote 18 sequels to *The Black Stallion* (and cowrote a 19th with his son).

10. Diablo—*The Cisco Kid* was based on O. Henry's story but wasn't exactly the same. In the original, Cisco was vicious, not Hispanic, and an outlaw.

11. Dollar—According to Hollywood legend, Wayne was so fond of Dollar that he requested no one else ride him.

**Good Breeding,
page 218**

**Tackle This!,
page 220**

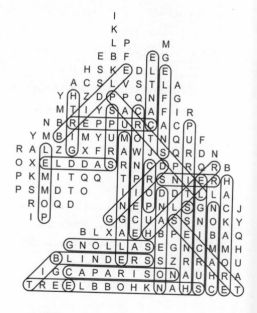

UNCLE JOHN'S BATHROOM READER:
FOR PET LOVERS

Find these and other great *Uncle John's Bathroom Reader* titles online at www.bathroomreader.com. Or contact us:

Bathroom Readers' Institute
PO Box 1117
Ashland, OR 97520
888.488.4642

The Last Page

S it down and be counted! Become a member of the Bathroom Readers' Institute! No join-up fees, monthly minimums or maximums, organized dance parties, quilting bees, solicitors, annoying phone calls (we only have one phone line), spam—or any other canned meat product—to worry about . . . just the chance to get our fabulous monthly newsletter and (if you want) some extremely cool Uncle John's stuff.

So check out our Web site: www.bathroomreader.com

Or send us a letter:
Uncle John's Bathroom Reader
Portable Press
10350 Barnes Canyon Road
San Diego, CA 92121

Or email us at unclejohn@btol.com.

Hope you enjoyed the book—and if you're skipping to the end, go back and finish!